Doubt on Trial

An Agnostic Minister's Case For Questioning the Bible

By
Rusty Williams

The Barefoot Ministries

To Elissa: You deserve all my love and gratitude. If I have flown just one foot off the ground it's only because you have encouraged me to soar and are the wind beneath my wings.

To Matt and Corey: You two unknowingly ignited my imagination all those years ago by allowing me to be your father. I could not be more proud of the men you've become.

Acknowledgements

This book began in my head more than ten years ago, and there are so many people who've influenced my life – and the writing of this book – during that time it would be impossible to name them all. As this last part of the book is concluding, I'm recovering from another concussion, my second in the last four months, and the seventh diagnosed concussion in the last twelve years. This is on top of a traumatic brain injury I suffered almost thirty years ago. To say that my memory isn't very good right now would be an understatement!

I am fearful of not being able to remember all the names of the people who are responsible for this book being written, and now published. I'm afraid I'll forget someone's name; that's the symptom I'm struggling with the most (more than once I've called one of our dogs my son's name and I've called my son our dog's name). I don't want to hurt anyone by not including their name in this acknowledgement.

So it is with a profound sense of humility and a heart filled with gratitude that I would like to thank my family – my immediate family and my extended family. You mean the world to me and without your presence in my life, this book would not have been possible. I wish there was a phrase more powerful than "thank you." Please know that I am grateful beyond words for you.

That humility and gratitude also includes my friends – friends who I've known most of my life, friends who I've known for just a little while, and those friends who I've only met by way of electronic media. Each of you has helped shape my opinions and beliefs, and you have helped nudge me to explore and to research. Thank you.

I owe a debt of gratitude to my mentors, to those people in my life who not only never gave up on me but encouraged me to go farther than I ever thought possible. From police officers who guided me as a kid looking for trouble, to teachers who pushed me, to professors who challenged me, and to those in the clergy who were role models for the kind of minister I dreamt of becoming: Each and every one of you helped guide my path and influence my world. Thank you.

And, to those authors who have invested countless hours into their own research so they could share their knowledge and wisdom with those who read their books, especially those authors who are mentioned in the *Recommended Reading* page of this book: I learned so much from your work, and much of what I've learned from you has been translated into my words so I could share them with those who read this book. Although we never met, and probably never will meet, know that your work matters and I am grateful for it.

All that being said, there is one person who deserves to be recognized for her work on the book: My editor, Sandy Sampson. You took the roughest of drafts and helped turn my thoughts and my words into something worth reading. Thank you for your countless hours devoted to this book, and especially for your friendship.

Rusty Williams
Medford Lakes, New Jersey
February 2021

Table of Contents

Chapter 1:

Pretrial Notes

Doubt

noun: a feeling of uncertainty or lack of confidence

verb: to be uncertain about

Doubt is one of those feelings that we know exists, but we have no way of proving it; that is, we can't identify it by its shape, size, color, or sound. All we know is that it's real – we've all felt it, we've all experienced it, and we know what it feels like when it's there inside our heads (or hearts). And yet, no doctor could ever identify it on an X-ray, nor find it if a patient was cut open on an operating room table. We know doubt is there, but it's not physically there; we know we've experienced it, but it can't be remembered the way we can record a vacation experience through photographs and videos.

Doubt can be both a blessing and a curse, don't you agree? There have been times when we've doubted something, and we went with that gut feeling and it paid off! Then, there have been times we doubted something (maybe our own abilities or self-worth), only to learn later that we lost out on a great opportunity or accomplishment. Doubt has been credited with saving lives and blamed on ruining relationships. And things can get even more confusing when we question our doubts – when we doubt our doubts. (Now, someone, somewhere, has got to be thinking that a double negative is a positive. If only it were that simple.)

Tangling Doubt and Faith

As confusing as doubt can be, there is one area where it comes with a nice serving of guilt as a side dish: faith. Perhaps nowhere is doubt more vilified than on the topic of faith. It seems that faith is one area where a good number of people believe you either have it or you don't – there is no in-between. And if you do express doubt, it's seen as a problem, as a lack of faith. It's almost as if faith can somehow be measured, and doubt brings that measurement down.

The same can be said with our faith beliefs: We either believe or we don't believe. There is no room for doubt when it comes to what we believe. Again, for a lot of people, it's a black or white issue; there is no gray area. And that means the gray matter we all possess is asked to look the other way if anything comes along that challenges what we believe.

> *Expressing doubt can be viewed as a lack of faith. It's almost as if faith can somehow be measured, and doubt brings that measurement down.*

Doubt is acceptable in most areas of life – just not in our faith lives, nor in our beliefs. It's as if there is a movement to eliminate doubt from our religions; after all, life in the Church would be so much easier (especially for the clergy) if doubt was turned away at the doors every Sunday morning. One wonders: If doubt had a pulse, if it was some kind of life matter, how many religious leaders would rather see its heart stop? If doubt was fighting to survive in the Church, would church leaders help it survive or hasten its demise? And if most people in the religious world would rather indict doubt as a villain than see it as a possible asset in our faith journeys, who in the faith community would be there to defend it? An agnostic minister, that's who!

2

Explaining a Minister's Agnosticism

Agnosticism

noun

a: the view that any ultimate reality (such as a deity) is unknown and probably unknowable; a philosophical or religious position characterized by uncertainty about the existence of a god or any gods

b: an attitude of doubt or uncertainty about something

Now, if the term "agnostic minister" seems like a paradox to you, don't fret – you're in good company. Well, you're in the company of someone who has doubts, someone who wonders, someone who questions, someone who researches, someone who was ordained into the Christian ministry more than twelve years ago – and that experience opened a door that has led to a journey that he wasn't expecting. Yep, I'm talking about the guy who is writing this as you're reading it: me.

And while I'm sure I'm not alone in my doubts and my questions, it sure can feel lonely. I'm comforted by knowing I am in good company. I know other members of the clergy who have doubts, or in some cases, have lost their faith altogether. So, yeah, I'm not alone, but identifying as an agnostic while at the same time having the title of minister can be a hard sell to anyone who asks. However, before you make any rash decisions about the author of this book, let me do my best to explain what it means to be an agnostic, and we'll let that explanation serve as a foundation on which this book was written.

The word *agnostic* comes from two Greek words: "gnosis" and the prefix "a." The word *gnosis* means knowledge (or information), and the prefix *a* means without. So, in terms of religion, an agnostic is a person without knowledge (without information, if you will) about God or things from God. Being agnostic isn't the same thing as being an atheist, which is a person who doesn't believe in God; rather,

3

agnosticism expresses the view that something is unknown or unknowable.

As this book moves forward, it will become apparent (if I've done my job) that there are things about God of which we lack knowledge. For example, some stories in the Bible contradict each other and history, and there are creeds and doctrines that were created outside of the teachings of Jesus. And you may already know that, rather than being created by just one writer, the books of the Bible were written by unknown authors.

As someone who lacks the knowledge about God and what was actually said by Jesus almost two thousand years ago, I simply feel I don't have enough information to say with definitive authority that what is written is what was said. So this book explores some of the sayings of Jesus that contradict each other. In particular, we consider things that Jesus said in one Gospel that contradict what he said in another Gospel.

As a person living in a time when I've always had access to TV news coverage that documented historical events and speeches, it's impossible to imagine what it was like living in early first-century Palestine where the literacy rate was between 3 and 5 percent, and the percentage of those who could write was less than half of that. So again, I can't say I have the knowledge necessary – the information I need – to make certain claims about the Bible and its contents.

I guess you might say that I have doubts. But I don't believe having doubts makes me less of a person than a Christian with rock-solid faith. I do believe that my time in seminary and my subsequent research afterward has guided me toward using critical-thinking skills instead of just accepting what I've been told, and have believed, since my days in Sunday school. And so, this book is about doubt.

But it's not going to be preachy. There are too many books out there (in my opinion) that seem overly preachy, and that way of delivering information has always been a turnoff for me. So I decided this book wouldn't be one of those preachy books that makes the author seem to know more than the reader and therefore delivers the information in a condescending manner. God knows, I don't have enough education to be an expert on anything, let alone religion. And I'm not trying to convince you of anything or to prove something; my goal isn't to convert or dissuade anyone of any beliefs they might have. I'm simply going to present information that is learned in almost every seminary and theological institution in the world – information that is taught to theology students, but rarely makes it out of the academic world to be presented to congregations.

This book is not a scholarly text intended to be used to prove or disprove anything in the theological realm of thinking, and it's certainly not written as a textbook for use in an educational setting. Instead, it is a book where doubt has its day in court.

Defending Doubt in Court

The format of this book is presented as a transcript of a criminal court case, where *Doubt* is on trial for its life. You see, the prosecution – on behalf of the plaintiff, The Church – wants to eradicate *Doubt*; the prosecution would like to put *Doubt* to death for what it's done to *Faith*. This book picks up at that point in the trial where the prosecution has rested its case after calling just one witness: The Church. The Church has testified both for its members and its clergy – after all, the Church often governs both of them. So the Church believes it has the authority to speak for its members and clergy, and in this case, give testimony for all concerned.

The defense will begin with an opening statement, followed by calling just one witness itself: *Doubt. Doubt* is testifying on its own behalf. And probably against the advice of its closest friends and loved ones, *Doubt* has hired an agnostic minister to present its defense. That agnostic minister is the author of this book. Again, much of what will be argued by the defense is taught in most seminaries and theological schools, and has been taught for hundreds of years. It's important that you, the reader of this book, understand that. Because you, the reader, are the jury.

Deciding Doubt's Fate

As the jury, it falls to you to ultimately decide if *Doubt* deserves to live or if *Doubt* should be put to death. After hearing the testimony of the defense's one witness, you will be asked to weigh that information against everything you know, everything you've thought, and everything bad you've been told about *Doubt*. As you hear the defense's case, I ask you to have an open mind and an open heart. And I would ask that you please set aside any preconceived ideas or beliefs you've been holding on to and allow yourself to act the part of an impartial juror – a person who is holding in their hands the fate of what the defense will argue is a misunderstood yet vital part of our critical religious thinking.

As a juror, you are free to now consider what type of courtroom you find yourself in. Think about that now – even, if you are able, imagine what the inside of that courtroom looks like. Is it a courtroom from the past, the kind of courtroom that might have been in the old Perry Mason TV show? Or, is it a newer, more modern type of courtroom that you might walk into today? Whatever you imagine, whatever you see in your mind's eye, that's your courtroom. Some readers won't actually see a courtroom, they'll just imagine one, and that's ok! If you don't see a courtroom, just think of a courtroom – that's your courtroom.

And in the same way, you can imagine what that jury box looks like and feels like. Where you're sitting right now is a seat in the jury box in that courtroom. What kind of vantage point do you have to the bench where the judge is sitting? Is the judge to your right as you're looking over there or is the judge to your left? If you were to scan the rest of the courtroom, is it crowded or are only a few people there? If there are people there, who are they? Do they represent an organization or business? Do they know the accused?

And finally, what about *Doubt*? When you think about *Doubt*, what do you imagine? If you don't see anything, or anyone, in your imagination, where do you feel *Doubt* in your own body? Where does

Doubt usually manifest itself when *Doubt* shows up in your life? I can't imagine anyone reading this far who hasn't had more than a few run-ins with *Doubt*.

Maybe you're wondering why I haven't painted a picture that details the courtroom and *Doubt*. Maybe you're glad I didn't! After all, this book isn't about me and my understanding of *Doubt*; instead, it's for you and *your* experiences with *Doubt*. I've found that the best way for someone to become interested in something as personal as *Doubt* is to allow themselves to experience it the way they see it and the way they feel it. I believe my job isn't to tell you *what* to think, but instead encourage you *to* think. Because, consider this possibility: Not everyone has positive memories when it comes to courtrooms. If I were to describe a courtroom that reminded you of a bad experience, how much more of this book would you read before you remembered different parts of that experience? And then I've lost you.

As will be mentioned more than a few times in the following pages, I don't want to tell you what to think, what beliefs to hold on to, or how you're supposed to respond. My intent is to offer information that allows you to create the picture in your mind that best allows you to experience the material the way you want to experience it. My hope is that by the end of this book, I will have accomplished that goal.

So, ladies and gentlemen of the jury, thank you for your time and interest in this landmark case. Let's get started.

Chapter 2:

The Defense's Opening Statement

*Reading the Bible * The Church and Doubt * A Historical Figure from the First Century*

The Church v. Doubt

Charge:	Doubt has endangered Faith
Plaintiff:	The Church (on behalf of its members and clergy)
Defense:	Doubt (defended by an agnostic minister)
The Court:	The Judge
Jury:	You, the Reader
Sentence:	Life or Death

The Court:

Defense counsel, are you ready to proceed?

Defense:

Yes, Your Honor, we are ready.

The Court:

The floor is yours.

Defense:

Thank you, Judge.

Ladies and gentlemen of the jury, you've heard all the negative things about my client. You've heard the Church's testimony about how *Doubt* has caused problems with it. You heard the Church tell stories about how *Doubt* has caused some of its members to leave – stories that paint a picture of worry for clergy as they admit they don't have all the answers to what *Doubt* causes in their congregations and to *Faith* as a whole.

Shortly, you are going to hear from *Doubt*. You're going to hear why my client's existence in the Church doesn't have to result in its members leaving. Instead, *Doubt* will explain why it came into being once laypeople were able to read the Bible without input from their church's leaders. And you'll see how by asking questions about what's in the Bible and the creeds, *Doubt* can elicit a deeper understanding of one's faith instead of diluting it.

One question that probably can't be answered is why the testimony you will hear hasn't been shared by the Church. The information *Doubt* will share with you has been taught in just about every seminary and place of theological learning in the world! Any clergy member would not view the testimony *Doubt* gives as blasphemous or heretical; in fact, most would probably accept it as a refresher for what they learned years ago. It's only the most fundamental of church leaders who might argue strongly that the information *Doubt* will share has somehow been taken out of context. The question that will be left unanswered is, "Why hasn't this material been shared by the Church?"

You see, the Church teaches the Bible from a devotional standpoint, and therefore, its members learn the Bible from that perspective. And it needs to be said upfront that there is nothing wrong with that – there is nothing wrong with reading the Holy Bible from a devotional or confessional standpoint. The Bible is, without question, the most influential book that has ever been written. It's a book that has transcended the generations for almost the last two thousand years.

However, if asked, how many of you – the members of the jury – can honestly say that you've read it? And when I say, "Read it," I mean cover to cover, from the first chapter of Genesis to the last chapter of Revelation. Hey, if I'm being honest with you – and I should since I am here representing the defendant – I can't say that one day I said to myself, "You know what, I think I'll sit down with the Bible today and start to read it." Like you, I can say I've *read* the Bible, but when I say that, I mean I've read passages from its various books at different times throughout my ministry. Most of us read a passage and then consider that passage from a devotional or confessional point of view.

So arguably the most important book that mankind has ever known is not read as often as we would like to think – as often as today's Church would want it to be read by its members. That, the defense concedes. But what if we asked the Church to encourage its members to read the Bible from a different point of view, to consider its contents with a different mindset? That is what I'm going to be asking of you, the members of the jury. I'm going to ask you to consider the testimony you will hear from *Doubt* with an open mind that is separate from the devotional way you've read or heard passages from the Bible. What you are being asked to do is to consider the words in the Bible from a historical perspective and with a critical mindset. When the Bible is read historically with a critical lens, its message becomes a different one than what we learned in Sunday school!

For the purpose of brevity, and to make sure this trial doesn't drag on for weeks, we're going to focus on only the New Testament. And we think you'll agree with us that the books of

> *Consider the words in the Bible from a historical perspective and read it with a critical mindset.*

the New Testament are much more familiar to us. Certainly, the Church would agree with us on this.

So where do we begin? In preparing for this trial, this question kept me awake at night – a lot of nights. Should we begin in the present time and work our way backward to the time when the New Testament was being written? Or, do we start when the Common Era began and move forward through the development of the Church? It seems my client *Doubt* has been there, no matter which direction we go.

After giving it much thought, I decided that we should begin with a noted story from history, a story that begins in the first century of the Common Era. This is the story of, who some called at the time, an unusual man who was born in the first century in an out-of-the-way part of the Roman Empire. His mother was visited by a heavenly being before he was born. She was told her son would become much more than an ordinary man – her son would be divine. And when he was born, his birth was accompanied by unusual heavenly signs.

As most men did at the time, he left his home when he became an adult. As an itinerant preacher, he went from village to village telling anyone who would listen that they shouldn't be concerned with their earthly lives or their possessions. He preached that they should live for what is spiritually eternal. As his preaching went on, he gathered more and more followers who became convinced that he was definitely more than an ordinary man – they came to believe that he was the Son of God. He performed miracles that confirmed their belief: He healed the sick, he cast out demons, and he raised the dead. His followers later described him as a man who led his life in an extraordinary and remarkable way.

It is well-documented that toward the end of his life he pissed off the authorities and was put on trial. But even though they killed his physical body, they couldn't kill his soul; so he ascended to Heaven where he continues to live for eternity. And there's proof that he lived on after leaving the earthly world: He appeared again to at least one of his followers, who was then convinced that he in fact still lived. And it is said he lives with us now. Later, after his physical death and ascension to Heaven, some of his followers wrote books about him, and those books have existed from when they were written until today.

I'm sure you can all guess who I'm talking about, right? Yep, if you guessed that first-century philosopher Apollonius of Tyana, you'd be correct! Apollonius was a Greek philosopher who lived in the first century, believed to have been born around the same time as Jesus.

I begin the defense of *Doubt* with this story to illustrate the importance of keeping an open mind during this trial and to remind us all how easy it is to fall into false assumptions when we hear something that sounds familiar to us. So again, I appeal to you to find a way to set aside any preconceived beliefs you hold about the Bible and allow my client to tell a different side of the story. I am convinced, as is *Doubt*, that when you make the decision to read the words in the Bible from a historical

> *When Doubt enters the room, keep an open mind and allow yourself to set aside preconceived notions about the Bible.*

standpoint and with a critical eye, you will indeed understand how and why my client needs to live.

Thank you.

Chapter 3:

Morning Testimony

*The Purpose of Doubt * Science and the Bible * The Old Testament * Canon of Scripture * Contradiction in the Book of Genesis * New Testament Issues * New Testament Writers * New Testament Slants and Sources*

The Court:

Counselor, call your witness.

Defense:

Thank you, Your Honor.

The defense calls as its witness, *Doubt.*

The Court:

Doubt, please raise your right hand. Do you swear that the testimony you are about to give will be the truth, the whole truth, and nothing but the truth?

Doubt:

I do, Your Honor.

The Court:

Defense counsel, you may proceed.

Defense:

Thank you, Judge.

Doubt, thank you for having the courage to take the witness stand and tell this jury why you're here and why, when it comes to the stories in the Bible, you seem to appear without warning and hang around in places you're not wanted – especially, in the Church.

What is your purpose in life?

Doubt:

My purpose? I see my purpose as one that causes people to question things when there are contradictions or improbabilities, to investigate and probe deeper. And here's what it's not: My purpose *is not* to try to get anyone to change their faith. Instead, I am present to encourage people to think, to use their God-given intelligence to consider facts when facts are there, and to consider what to make of something when facts aren't there.

I don't have a horse in this race; that is, I'm not here to make someone think a certain way about a topic – especially when it comes to faith. I'm here to create that certain gut feeling when something doesn't seem right. I know I can be a downer sometimes, but I also know my purpose is a noble one, and I'm sure I've saved many lives because of the feelings I've created in people who were about to do something foolish or even dangerous.

I think the theologian Frederick Buechner described me best when he said, "If you don't have doubts, you're either kidding yourself or asleep. Doubts are the ants in the pants of faith.

15

They keep us awake and moving." Hopefully, my testimony keeps the members of the jury awake and moving. At the very least, I hope my testimony here gives them reasons to think and consider information that they might not have been aware of before this trial started. (However, I don't see the need to put ants in their pants.)

And I want to repeat that I am not here to create a belief or a nonbelief. And when it comes to religion, to someone's faith, I want to make sure everyone knows that I don't want to change anyone's beliefs. When it comes to a person's most intimate beliefs, such as faith, I do not become present to change their faith. I'm just there, sitting there wherever that feeling is in their body, waiting to be opened or to be ignored. And it doesn't matter to me if I'm ignored or acted on. I swear, as sure as I'm sitting here with you, it doesn't matter to me — you are not going to hurt my feelings if you ignore me, nor are you going to boost my ego if you act on me. I'm simply here as a resource if someone chooses to use me.

Defense:

So are you saying that it was when the idea of faith began in the human story, perhaps when the Bible was starting to be written, that your presence became known?

Doubt:

No, sir, not at all. When you think about how long ago it was that human civilization began compared to when the first books of the Bible were written, it's obvious I've been around long before there was any known discussion of faith. However, that's not to say that religion, faith, and the books of the Bible haven't all brought me to the forefront.

Defense:

What do you mean?

Doubt:

Well, we know from science that the earth is at least four billion years old, and—

Defense:

Whoa, wait a minute there. Are you talking science in a discussion about faith?

Doubt:

Oh, boy, here we go. Look, there is no reason science and faith, science and religion – science and God – can't be talked about in the same discussion. The way I see it, the same God that gave us brains would probably appreciate it if we used them. It never ceases to amaze me how people will question the results of scientific studies but accept as pure truth something that was written thousands of years ago and not even think to question it.

> *When considering science and faith, the same God that gave us brains would probably appreciate it if we used them.*

Science tells us that the earth is at least four billion years old. Some people who read the Bible claim the world is less than ten thousand years old. Think about that for a minute: Some people are relying on what was written thousands of years ago to come to a conclusion about the age of the earth. But there was no scientific method back then, no real understanding of biology or science – at least, not the same understanding that we have today.

For example, during the time when the books of the Bible were written, it was believed, and accepted as truth, that a man planted his seed inside a woman, causing a baby to grow inside her. The understanding of that day was that a man's sperm was actually seed, like the seed that was planted into the ground to grow crops. People's understanding was that a man's seed was planted into a woman during sex and the woman's only role was to act as an incubator of sorts, fertile soil if you will, for the seed to mature into a fully formed human baby that was expelled about nine months after the act of sex. It wasn't until the invention of the microscope at the end of the sixteenth century that human cells were seen for the first time, and then another ninety years after that before the microscope was used to discover the connection between spermatozoa from men and the egg from women.

Oh, crap, I am allowed to talk about sperm in court, aren't I?

Defense:

Yes, you can discuss sperm in court. I'm sure the members of the jury have heard it before.

Doubt:

Okay, good. I was afraid I might have pissed off someone, especially the judge, and I don't want to do that. I'm pretty sure I'm going to be pissing off people later on with my testimony anyway.

Defense:

Umm, *Doubt* – while it's okay to say sperm in court, "piss" is something you should try to refrain from saying.

Doubt:

Good to know. I guess it's a good thing I said, "Oh, crap," instead of, "Oh, shit," earlier, huh?

The Court:

Counselor, may I suggest that you move on so we don't end up with the jury hearing about every bodily function.

Defense:

Yes, Judge; of course.

Doubt, let's get back to the age of the earth. I believe you were talking about that before we got sidetracked.

Doubt:

Sorry about that.

Like I was saying, the earth is at least four billion years old and humans have existed on it, living in civilizations, for the last six million years. So it seems to reason that if humans have been around for six million years, and the first books of the Bible – the Old Testament – were written about three thousand years ago, I was here long before even the ancient writings of the Torah.

Defense:

The Torah? Can you tell the members of the jury what the Torah is?

Doubt:

The first five books of the Old Testament are often referred to as the Torah. These books are called the Torah because they contain the law given by God. The word *Torah* means instruction, teaching, or law in Hebrew.

Historians and anthropologists believe the first books of the Bible were written about a thousand years before the Common Era – that is, about a thousand years before the birth of Jesus. The books of the Bible cover about fifteen hundred years of ancient history. And here's where I first come into play – when religion and faith are discussed or even thought about.

There are people who say that the earth is roughly six thousand years old; these are the people who rely on what's written in the Bible instead of trusting science. And since the earth is only six thousand years old, and Jesus lived about two thousand years ago, then the Bible covers a historical period of four thousand years. They believe the Bible covers everything from the beginning of time until the end of Jesus' life.

When science and faith clash, I seem to appear out of nowhere. When the judge asked me if I swore to the tell the truth, I swore to the tell the truth as I know it using critical-thinking skills and listening to what scientists, anthropologists, and historians have to say. It wasn't easy, but I've learned how to look at scientific, historical, and anthropological teachings without allowing my faith beliefs to disrupt my thinking and thereby distort the facts.

It's like what you told the jury in your opening statement: I can either consider things from a devotional and religious place of understanding or I can consider things from a perspective where I evaluate facts as they are presented to me. It's hard; I know it's hard. But if I'm going to be honest with myself, I must set aside my religious beliefs when I'm asked to think about facts. That doesn't mean I give up my religious beliefs. It just means I set them aside, so they don't influence rational thought when facts are in front of me.

Defense:

Let's go back to something you said, and I think you might have referred to it earlier. You've referred to time periods as being in the Common Era or before the Common Era. I know you briefly mentioned what they are, but I want to make sure the jury understands those terms. Can you tell the jury what is meant by the terms the *Common Era* and *before the Common Era?*

Doubt:

Sure. Looking back in history, scholars say if it was a date before Christ was born, it was abbreviated as B.C. for *before*

Christ. And the period in history from the time of Jesus' birth forward is abbreviated as A.D., which is a Latin abbreviation for *anno Domini*, meaning *in the year of the Lord.*

In the academic world, and secular world for that matter, those abbreviations have been replaced with B.C.E., meaning *before the Common Era;* and C.E., meaning the *Common Era.* Using math and a whole lot of research found in the Gospels, experts have been able to work backwards from the Crucifixion though the history of the ruling leaders of the Roman Empire to date the birth of Jesus to be around 4 B.C.E.

Defense:

And you testified earlier that the first books of the Old Testament were written around a thousand years before the birth of Jesus, is that right?

Doubt:

Yes, give or take a hundred years or so. So the time those books were written would be 1000 B.C.E. And I also said that the Bible itself covers about fifteen hundred years of history. According to those who study it from an academic perspective, the books of the Bible cover the history of the Jewish people and the lands they lived in from about 1400 B.C.E. until 100 C.E. Again, give or take a couple hundred years in either direction.

Defense:

And here we are, almost two thousand years after the last book of the Bible was written, trying to figure out what was said and done in that ancient age. So can we assume that since it's documented in the Bible, we have accurate information on that time period?

Doubt:

Unfortunately, no, that's not right.

21

Defense:

> Why is that? Why can't we say that information in the Bible is accurate?

Doubt:

> To start with, we don't know who wrote the books of the Bible. Well, we don't know who wrote all but a few books in the Bible, and those books are in the New Testament.
>
> Maybe I should start with what the Bible is. The Bible is a collection of books, written thousands of years ago, that have become known as sacred texts in different religions. I know you want to stay focused on the New Testament, but I think the jury should know that experts in their fields – those who teach at universities and seminaries – say we simply have no way of knowing who wrote most of the books that are in the Bible. (By the way, the word *Bible* is Greek for "the books." So we have a collection of books in a book called, "The Books." I always found it interesting that the best-selling book of all time is a book of books called, "The Books.")

Defense:

> We may not know who wrote them, but at least we know the books of the Bible are historically accurate for the time periods in which they were written, right?

Doubt:

> Again, unfortunately, no – we can't say the books of the Bible are historically accurate. There are too many contradictions, too many differences in books telling the same story, and too many instances where the descriptions of events in the Bible are at odds with what we have from history books outside the canon of the Bible.

Defense:

Let's stop for a minute, before we go further into that. You said the canon of the Bible. Would you explain to the jury what you mean by canon?

Doubt:

Well, it doesn't mean a large gun that fires big round projectiles at the enemy, if that's what you're asking! Although, it has been used – I should say, it has been *abused* – to assault people who think differently than what certain churches believe to be true.

The canon I'm referring to has one *n* in it, the big gun cannon has two *n's* in it. Anyway, the word canon in religious circles means the accepted authoritative scripture. Early Christians took the word from Greek and Hebrew and gave it the meaning "rule of faith." When referring to the Bible, it can be said the books of the Bible are the *canonical books* of scripture – meaning, the accepted authoritative books. There were a lot of other books written in parallel times as some of the books of the Bible were being written, but they didn't make it into the Bible; you could say, they didn't make the final cut. These books are referred to as *noncanonical books*, meaning they have some theological relevance, but the Church authorities found them to be unacceptable (for a variety of reasons) to be included with the books of the Bible. Another way to describe these books is they are books outside the canon of scripture.

Defense:

Thank you for clearing that up. Now, moving on to your assertion that we can't say the books of the Bible are historically accurate: You mentioned contradictions, differences, and historical problems. Can you elaborate on that?

Doubt:

> And here is where I made a big splash in the study of the Bible – by scholars and laypeople alike!
>
> Oh, boy, where to begin?
>
> I know you asked me to stick with the New Testament, but for a quick example, can I go back to the Old Testament? It will be really quick, I promise.

The Court:

> Make it quick, *Doubt*. Both sides have agreed to focus on the New Testament; I'll allow you to give an example but keep it short.

Doubt:

> I will, Your Honor.

Defense:

> Okay, *Doubt*, you were starting to say—

Doubt:

> All anyone has to do to see that there are contradictions in the Bible is open the first book of it, the Book of Genesis. And you don't have to read past the second chapter. Most people, if you ask them, will tell you they are familiar with the story of Adam and Eve and the Garden of Eden. What I've learned over the years is that it's not widely known that there are two creation stories in the Book of Genesis. There's a story of creation in the first chapter of Genesis and another story in the second chapter of Genesis. And there are differences in those stories.

Defense:

What do you mean by differences?

Doubt:

To begin with, how God is referred to. In the first chapter, God is referred to as "God." As in "God created the heavens and the earth." In the second chapter, God is referred to as "the LORD God," as in "the LORD God formed man from the dust of the ground."

The second chapter consistently refers to God with the divine name "Yahweh." Bible translations translate that to be "the LORD" in all capitalized letters.

Defense:

Okay, but that's not that big of a deal. Are there any other contradictions that prove your point?

Doubt:

Oh, yeah; I'm just getting started.

Here's a question: Which did God create first, humans or animals? It depends on what chapter of Genesis you read. In the first chapter, we're told God created all the animals and then finally he created humankind. In the second chapter, God creates man and then he creates all the animals. Then, seeing that all the animals didn't give man companionship – that is, man was lonely without a helper or partner – God made a woman from the man's rib. And this woman would be man's partner and helper, and she would be man's companion.

Another question: How long did it take God to create everything? Again, it depends on which chapter you read. In the first chapter of Genesis, we read the familiar six-day story; that God created everything in the universe in six days and he rested on the seventh day. But the second chapter infers it took just one day: "On the day that the LORD God made the earth and the heavens."

What most people do is take what they've heard from the six-day creation story in chapter 1 and add the story of the rib taken from Adam in chapter 2, then put them together and believe they understand the creation story. But the truth is, they've created their own creation story by combining what they remember from chapter 1 and what they remember from chapter 2.

> *Most people create their own creation story by combining what they remember of stories in chapter 1 and chapter 2 of Genesis.*

Then there's the problem of what we know about the universe, what we know about astronomy, and how things work with the earth, the moon, and the sun. We know from our days in school that our sun is in fact a star. We learned that the earth not only rotates around the sun, giving us the seasons, but it also spins on its axis – giving us day and night. It's daylight on the part of the earth facing the sun, and its nighttime on the other side. And we know from science that it's the sun that provides the light. No arguments so far, right?

In the first chapter of Genesis, the story of creation tells us that on the first day God spoke, he said, "Let there be light." And there was light, and God saw that the light was good, and God separated the light from the darkness, and he called the light day and the darkness night. On the fourth day, God created the stars; we're told these were great lights – the greater light ruled the day, and the lesser lights ruled the night. We can assume that the greater light was referring to the sun.

Going back to our school days, we know that our sun is a star. It would seem that whoever wrote the first chapter of Genesis didn't understand what we learned in grade school. But even more telling is that there was light before the creation of the sun. If the sun gives us light, how is it that there was light before the very thing that gives us light was created?

I think now you can begin to understand how I made a splash in the minds of scholars and laypeople who have been trying to figure out these problems in the very first book of the Bible. People come up with theological explanations for the differences and contradictions, but those explanations are based on faith – not on what we know from the world of science and what was more likely to have happened.

Defense:

Okay, let's move on to the New Testament.

Doubt:

Can I say one more thing about the Book of Genesis? Just one more thing, I swear. It is what is taught by scholars and what's discussed in seminaries around the world.

Defense:

Go ahead.

Doubt:

Okay, this is probably going to ruffle some feathers. Scholars using a textual criticism technique known as the Documentary Hypothesis have determined that the second chapter of Genesis was written *before* the first chapter.

Defense:

What? Did you just say that the second chapter in the Book of Genesis was written before the first chapter?

Doubt:

That's what biblical scholars who spend most of their careers researching and studying this stuff say. According to them, the second chapter of Genesis was probably written around 922 B.C.E. and the first chapter was probably written around 539 B.C.E. So there's a gap of four hundred years between the two chapters – which means there's a gap of four hundred years between the two creation stories. And that's when it begins to make sense why there are the differences in them that I pointed out earlier.

Biblical scholars believe the two creation accounts were traditions from different periods in ancient Israel. These traditions were thought to be the way people living in different parts of Israel in those times understood humanity and God. And I should make it clear that scholars aren't saying neither story is true. There's no way to prove that they didn't happen the way they're described in Genesis. Scholars, just like me, have no interest in trying to prove whether there is a God or there isn't a God; or, if there is a God, what kind of God he (or she) is and what God did in the past. Biblical scholars and experts in anthropology and ancient history are driven to determine what most likely happened based on all the evidence they have.

Defense:

And you said this is taught in seminaries? If that's the case, why haven't we heard about it until now?

Doubt:

I can't answer the second part of your question. It could be that the Church isn't comfortable with it. Think about it: The Church has taught the creation story for centuries now and for them to suddenly tell their congregations, "We have something to share with you…" might cause people to leave. It would surely cause dissension.

As for the first part of your question, yes: Most mainstream Christian seminaries teach everything I've just talked about regarding the Book of Genesis to their students. And then, those students are taught the theological side of it – how to interpret it through the lens of faith. So they have answers that explain the discrepancies. But most clergy members never have to consider these facts after they're ordained for the simple reason that they are never brought up in church.

Defense:

I wonder if the members of the jury were aware of these facts. Let's move on to the New Testament.

Doubt:

But there are a bunch of discrepancies and contradictions in other books of the Old Testament that I think you should know, especially between the books First Kings and Chronicles. Let me just—

The Court:

No way, *Doubt! Doubt*, you promised that you'd keep it short and only talk about Genesis. Counselor, move on to the New Testament.

Doubt:

But, Judge, you don't understand. If you just let me explain a few more things—

The Court:

Doubt, unless you want to find a way to come up with bail money after I find you in contempt of court, I suggest you listen to the next question from your lawyer and not argue with me. Do you want to be held in contempt of court?

Doubt:

No, not yet. There's gonna be plenty of opportunity for that as this trial proceeds.

Defense:

Judge, I apologize for my client's behavior. *Doubt* can sometimes get louder and more intense as questions become deeper and more controversial.

Doubt, I'm sure the jury gets it: If there are contradictions in the first two chapters of the first book in the Bible, it stands to reason that there are more contradictions and problems in the rest of the books. So let's accept the fact that other books in the Old Testament have problems and move on to the New Testament.

Doubt:

I'm sorry, sometimes once I get going, it's hard to stop me. Sure, the New Testament. Whatcha got for me?

Defense:

In your opinion, are there similar problems in the books of the New Testament as those in the Old Testament?

Doubt:

Yes. And I think those problems are even more problematic.

Defense:

How are they more problematic?

Doubt:

They're more problematic because of the nature of the New Testament. It's not that they occur at higher rates than in the Old Testament; it's because the New Testament is based solely on the words, teachings, and actions of one person – Jesus. The Old Testament is a collection of books containing the words, teachings, and actions of multiple characters, most of them called prophets. The New Testament is linear-focused on Jesus and what he preached.

Christianity is based on just one person – Jesus, who was the Christ. The word *Christ* is Greek for "the anointed one." That's where the word Christian comes from; a Christian is someone who follows the teachings of Jesus Christ – Jesus, the anointed one. It's one thing to question the authority of ancient writings of the prophets of the Old Testament and the written history it portends. It's quite another thing, for the Church, to have the authority of the writings describing the life of Jesus questioned. For whatever their reasons, questioning the historical accuracy of the New Testament is often considered sacrilegious to Christians and, in a global sense, the Church.

Defense:

Can you elaborate on some of the problems in the New Testament that prevent us from being able to call it historically accurate?

Doubt:

That's my main reason for being here, isn't it?

The best way to explain them is to first explain what the New Testament is and how and when it was written.

The word *testament* comes from the Latin word *testamentum*. It is generally accepted that this means covenant or agreement. Some claim that in the context of the Bible, the word testament means promise.

The New Testament is a collection of twenty-seven books, as they're called, describing the birth, ministry, and death of Jesus, as well as letters from some of his apostles; an account of the works of the earliest apostles; and finally, a revelation. These books were written over a period of about fifty years, beginning about twenty years after the Crucifixion of Jesus.

Defense:

Wait, you're saying that the first writings about Jesus didn't occur until twenty years after his death? I thought the Gospels were written by eyewitnesses who were there with Jesus during his ministry.

Doubt:

You wouldn't be the first one to think that!

The fact is, the first Gospel to be written wasn't written until at least forty years after the Crucifixion. But the first Christian writings came from an apostle of Jesus, a man named Paul, who wrote a series of letters beginning about twenty years after the Crucifixion. I'll get back to Paul in a little bit.

Let me first start with the Gospels since most people are more familiar with the stories in them.

Here's the backdrop to Jesus' ministry: Jesus is widely thought to have been an itinerant preacher from the area of Palestine in the Roman empire. In early first-century Palestine, it is widely accepted that between 3 and 5 percent of the population was literate. Those who were literate – that is, they knew how to read – were part of the upper class, who would have been living in the more urban areas; Jesus preached in the rural areas. It's important to understand that back then, reading and writing were not taught at the same time. People who had enough money were taught to read, and if they had enough money to go on with their education, they were taught to write. It's believed that less than half the people who knew how to read also knew how to write. So we're talking about a very small portion of people knowing how to read and write.

The language common to the area of the empire where Jesus preached was Aramaic. The official language of the empire was Greek, but the people in the area where Jesus grew up, where he lived, where he preached, and where he died, had a language of their own – Aramaic. Everyone who Jesus ministered to spoke Aramaic. It is important to understand this because the Gospels were originally written in Greek, and they were written in a highly developed form of Greek. Greek was a language that Jesus would not have spoken.

> *Jesus preached in the Aramaic language to people who most likely could neither read nor write. The Gospels and every other book of the New Testament were written in Greek – forty or more years after Jesus' Crucifixion.*

It's also important to understand that the followers of Jesus – his disciples – were all from the same area and none of them is reported to have been educated. Most scholars agree that none of them would have been able to read or write. We can certainly deduce that those who were day laborers and fishermen would not have known how to read or write.

So right off the bat we have a language problem: Jesus, his followers, disciples, and those he interacted with all spoke Aramaic and were not literate; but the Gospels were all originally written in highly developed Greek, a language neither Jesus nor his disciples spoke.

I'd also like to add that it wasn't just the Gospels that were originally written in Greek; every book in the New Testament was originally written in Greek.

Defense:

Thank you for informing us of that. Go on.

Doubt:

As I said earlier, Jesus is believed to have been crucified around the year 30 C.E. Even though it doesn't appear as the first Gospel in the New Testament, the first Gospel written is the Gospel according to Mark, or simply, Mark. The person known as Mark was believed to have been a companion to the disciple Peter.

Most biblical scholars, historians, and anthropologists believe Mark's Gospel was written around the year 70 C.E. – meaning it was written at least forty years after the death of Jesus. The next Gospel written was Matthew, then Luke, and finally John. Matthew's Gospel is believed to have been written early in the ninth decade, probably around 82 or 83 C.E. Luke's Gospel was written late in the ninth decade, perhaps 87 to 89 C.E. And John's Gospel was written in the middle to the end of the tenth decade, say 96 to 98 C.E.

Matthew was a tax collector and one of the twelve disciples of Jesus. Luke was believed to be a physician who was a friend of the apostle Paul. And John was a fisherman and one of Jesus' twelve disciples.

By the way, in both the theological and the academic worlds, as well as in the Bible, these Gospels are called, "The Gospel according to…." If I were to be textually correct, I would be saying, "The Gospel according to Mark, The Gospel according to Matthew, The Gospel according to Luke, and The Gospel according to John." I just find that saying the name first rolls off my tongue easier. So for this trial, I'll be saying, "Mark's Gospel, Matthew's Gospel, Luke's Gospel, and John's Gospel." I just find it easier to say them that way.

Defense:

Earlier you mentioned the apostle Paul. When did Paul write his letters?

Doubt:

Paul wrote most of his letters in the sixth decade, with some going into the early seventh decade.

34

However, it's important to point out that some letters are attributed to Paul that scholars are certain were written after the Gospels, as late as the early part of the second century. That's because most scholars believe only seven of his thirteen letters are unquestionably authentic, meaning, they are sure he wrote those seven. The other six letters are called the *disputed letters* from Paul. They are probably forgeries. Of those six, there is some dispute among scholars as to whether Paul might have written two of them, but scholars are almost unanimous that at least four of them are forgeries.

Defense:

Wait a minute, are you saying the Bible contains forgeries?

Doubt:

That's what I'm saying. And not just letters from Paul. But this could take us on a tangent that I'm not sure we're going to have time for. Maybe we can come back to these if time allows.

Defense:

Great suggestion. Let's continue with the New Testament. If the Gospels weren't written until forty to seventy years after Jesus was killed, how do we know if they're accurate?

Doubt:

There you go, doing my job for me!

The fact is we have no way of knowing how accurate they are. We have to acknowledge that the Gospels are books that were written decades after the events they document, written in a language that neither Jesus nor his disciples spoke, by men who did not know Jesus.

There are a couple of reasons why I say that. The first is we can be certain that men wrote the books of the Bible; women were not permitted to be educated enough to read and write, so they were not the ones writing anything in antiquity. Second, the writers would not have known Jesus because, as I said earlier, the Gospels were all written in highly developed Greek; only the elite would have enough money to be able to be taught how to read and write, and those people lived nowhere near where Jesus preached. Finally, the average life span of men in the first century was less than fifty years. Since the first Gospel was written forty years after the Crucifixion, it is unlikely the

> *Each Gospel was written to paint Jesus in a certain light; they were each written with an agenda to try to describe who Jesus was.*

grown men who would have known Jesus – men around the same age as Jesus when he was preaching – would still be alive when the Gospels were written.

Since the people did not know how to read or write, they relied on oral traditions for lessons in their faith. And that faith was Judaism. Jesus was a Jew who taught Jewish law and maintained the Jewish customs. It was common for stories to be told that shared a larger truth about a topic. Meaning in order for something to be learned, a story was developed that made that truth come to life. Examples of this kind of storytelling are the parables Jesus taught. Jesus taught in parables because they not only drove the points home, they were the custom of that time.

Stories about Jesus were passed from synagogue to synagogue and then from generation to generation until someone – probably a wealthy man from a synagogue outside of Palestine – wrote down what was being shared in his synagogue. By the time the first Gospel was written, specific teachings of Jesus were already being discussed in small groups of synagogues – probably based on their geographic locations. So the teachings that were attributed to Peter's friend Mark were being shared in certain synagogues, while the teachings attributed to Matthew were being shared in other synagogues, and so on.

So by the time the first teachings of Jesus were written down, stories about both Jesus and his ministry had been circulating by word of mouth for generations. And those stories – in addition to an unknown source that scholars refer to as Q, for a German word meaning source – were the sources for what is in the Gospels.

Additionally, each Gospel was written to paint Jesus in a certain light. They were each written with an agenda to try to describe who Jesus was. Let me explain.

It is widely accepted that the author of Mark's Gospel wanted to emphasize that Jesus was the Messiah – the chosen one. Matthew's Gospel was written with an emphasis that not only was Jesus the new Messiah, he was also the new Moses. Luke's Gospel emphasized the universalism of the good news of Jesus – that the good news wasn't limited to Jews; gentiles could also receive it. And the writers of John's Gospel wrote to show how divine Jesus was; in fact, it is the only Gospel where Jesus says he and God are the same.

Defense:

Wait, did you misspeak when you said the "writers" of John's Gospel – writers as in plural, more than one?

Doubt:

I didn't slip; I did indeed say "writers." Scholars are fairly certain that at least two people wrote John's Gospel – maybe even three.

Defense:

To be sure, you are saying we don't know who wrote the Gospels.

Doubt:

No, we don't. They were all written anonymously. None of the Gospels are credited with authorship by anyone. Names were not attributed to them until around 200 C.E.; that is, their manuscripts weren't titled *Matthew*, *Mark*, *Luke*, and *John* until more than a century after they were first written.

Defense:

So to be sure we completely understand it now: The Gospels are books written anywhere from forty to seventy years after the death of Jesus, in a language neither Jesus nor his disciples spoke, by unknown – or anonymous – authors who never met or heard Jesus speak?

Doubt:

These are the authoritative books that document the life of Jesus and on which Christianity is based. And they are exactly as you just described them.

The Court:

Counselor, the jury has been in their seats for a while now. I think it would be a good idea if we took a short break and let them stretch their legs and get a snack or something to drink.

Defense:

That sounds like a good idea, Judge.

The Court:

Okay, then. We'll take a twenty-minute break, and when we return, the defense will continue its examination of *Doubt*.

Chapter 4:

Midmorning Testimony

*Manuscripts and the Scribes Who Copied Them * Manuscript Additions *
Manuscript Changes * The Word of God * New Testament Contradictions*

The Court:

Welcome back, ladies and gentlemen of the jury. Hopefully, you stretched your legs, had a chance to use the bathroom, and maybe grabbed a snack or something to drink.

Counselor, if you're ready, you can continue with your examination of *Doubt*.

Defense:

Yes, Your Honor, we're ready to continue.

Doubt, just before we broke for lunch, you were testifying about the Gospels. We don't know who wrote them, there was a wide gap in time before they were written, they were originally written in a language Jesus and his disciples didn't speak, and the writers never met Jesus.

I think the members of the jury would agree that all of this information gives us a lot of reasons to understand and appreciate the need for you in the world. But there's more information you can share that will solidify your position, isn't there?

Doubt:

Yes, there is a lot more.

Let me begin by sharing something I probably should have mentioned when we first started talking about the Bible. When people ask if I believe in the Bible, my response usually leaves them with a puzzled look on their faces. My reply to that question is, "Which Bible?"

People look at me as if I just asked them the stupidest question ever posed; in fact, some come right out and say that. I tell them they need to be more specific about which *version* of the Bible they're referring to. While there are a few who answer that question with an answer that confirms they've at least read the inside cover that states which version it is, many don't remember that there are multiple versions of the Bible.

I wonder if you, the members of the jury, know how many English-translated versions of the Bible there are. Some of you might think there are dozens of versions; others might think there could be around a hundred versions; and maybe a few of you think there are more than a hundred versions. I'm betting you'll be surprised to learn that there have been more than 450 versions of the Bible translated into English. And how each version got to make it to print is a hot topic for biblical scholars.

Taking just the New Testament into account, there are no original manuscripts; we, as a society, have no original manuscripts. They've been lost to the ages. We don't have first copies of the originals either. Nor do we have copies of the first copies. What we do have – that is, what is archived in museums and churches, as well as universities – are copies of copies of copies of some copy.

And remember, there were no photocopiers when these manuscripts were first written and then copied. Staples and Office Depot were not established as businesses in the first, second, third, and fourth centuries. In fact, the printing press wasn't invented until the middle of the fifteenth century. So the only way to copy a manuscript was to do it by hand.

Let's say a church leader in a town in Greece heard about the manuscript that was the Gospel of Mark, and he liked the teachings in it so much that he wanted a copy for his church. He would ask for a copy of it to be sent to him. The people charged with making copies of manuscripts were scribes. Ancient scribes were trained in copying manuscripts, letter by letter, line by line, page by page. These scribes were human; they weren't superhumans with special powers. They were regular people, just like you and me; their job – their career – in their town was to copy manuscripts.

Maybe you can see where problems arose.

Since scribes were human, they made mistakes. If mistakes were made in the manuscript, which was made for that church leader in Greece, he would have no way of knowing about the mistakes because he had nothing with which to compare that manuscript. Maybe there was another church leader in a different part of the empire who wanted a copy of Mark; he, too, would request a copy be sent to him. So a scribe would make a copy of Mark for him and send it away. Now this church leader has a copy of the Gospel of Mark with different mistakes than the church leader's manuscript in Greece. Neither church leader would know about the mistakes, and they would assume they had a good copy of the Gospel of Mark.

Taking this further, if other churches heard that the two church leaders I mentioned were getting really good feedback from their copies of the Gospel of Mark, those churches would ask for

Scribes weren't superhuman. In addition to mistakes in grammar, spelling, or formatting, they sometimes added or omitted text.

copies of the manuscript. Now other scribes were hired to do the copying, and since they were also human, they made a mistake or two. Now we have copies that have multiple mistakes in them. And this pattern continued until the invention of the printing press. Although, to be fair, mistakes were found faster since there were older manuscripts available to compare them to. It also needs to be said that most of the mistakes — the vast majority of them, like 95 percent — were mistakes in grammar or spelling or formatting. But the other 5 percent of the mistakes changed the manuscripts so that there are discrepancies that make me, *Doubt*, show up just like [*snaps fingers*] that.

It gets better. Or, worse, depending on how you're looking at it. Let's say a really good scribe gets his hands on a copy of a manuscript that he's been asked to make another copy of. In transcribing the manuscript, this scribe notices an error made by a prior scribe. This good scribe either makes a correction to the copy he's writing, so that there are now two manuscripts that differ from each other. Or, the scribe might make a notation in the margin of the one he's writing or the one he's copying from. Time goes on, and a different scribe gets his hands on the manuscript with the notation in the margin. Often, these scribes would include the notation in the piece they're working on. So now you have a copy of the text with at least two additions to the line where the mistake was originally made. Scholars have found this occurring many times when they've examined ancient copies of the manuscripts.

As this process continued through the decades of the centuries, church fathers in the third and fourth centuries, maybe as early as the second century, had to determine which manuscripts to use as they began to gradually construct the canon of the New Testament. As time went on, and the New Testament was established, the ones charged with putting the books together had to decide which manuscripts best documented what really happened and what was actually said.

More problems developed as the Bible was printed in various versions. The early Church claimed a certain version was the only accepted version; that the manuscripts used were the best manuscripts to create the Gospels that would become part of the New Testament. However, after that version of the Bible began to be circulated, older, more accurate, manuscripts were discovered. These manuscripts, scholars argue, are more accurate and therefore are better sources for the Gospels to be transcribed. So a new version was made. And then more manuscripts were found, and this process continued.

As time went on, some church leaders were arguing the version of the Gospels they had were the best; they said they were the most accurate. Leaders from other churches disagreed, saying they had the most accurate version of the Bible based on the manuscripts used to write the Gospels. And this went on for some time. Then, other theologians and scholars wanted to create versions of the Bible that used language that was more current to that time, using words and phrases that would be used in that time instead of antiquated ones. The King James version of the Bible comes to mind.

And so it continued until there were more than 450 versions of the Bible translated into English. That's just translated into English! So when I respond to the question, "Do you believe in the Bible?" with the question, "Which Bible?" I'm not just trying to be a smartass.

Defense:

Doubt, if I hear you right, you're saying scribes were only human, so they made mistakes. And those mistakes were copied, and other mistakes were made. Then, some mistakes were corrected, but those corrections sometimes only added to the confusion. Then, different versions of the Bible started to come out, with different sides saying they had the most accurate version. Is that how we got the Bible that we have today?

Doubt:

It's the beginning of how we got to the Bible we have today. There's more.

Not only did scribes make accidental mistakes, scholars have discovered that some of the changes to the manuscripts appear to be purposeful. Some scribes changed events because they believed what was in the manuscript didn't depict Jesus the way the original writer was trying to do. These changes included adding words as well as deleting words.

Let me give you three examples where scholars are certain a scribe added words to the manuscript to adapt it to what they thought it should be.

The first example is John's Gospel. It's a well-known passage, usually called, "The woman taken in adultery." It begins the eighth chapter of the Gospel [John 8:1-11]. It's the story where a woman who was caught in the act of adultery was brought before Jesus. Those who brought her asked Jesus what should be done to her. The law called for her to be stoned to death, but Jesus preached forgiveness. Those who brought this woman to Jesus did so to test him to see if he would keep the law from Moses or if he would want her forgiven and set free. Jesus saw it as a test and famously said, after scribbling something in the dirt with a stick, "Let the one who is without

44

sin cast the first stone." The ones who brought the woman to Jesus left the scene one by one, leaving just the woman and Jesus. Jesus asks the woman if there is no one left to condemn her. The woman replies no, and Jesus tells her, "Neither do I condemn you. Go and sin no more."

Biblical scholars agree that this passage was a later addition, written in by a scribe who probably heard the story or something similar in the area of the empire where he lived. This scribe either added it in the margin as a way to describe the nature of Jesus or intentionally put it into the manuscript to begin the chapter. Scholars know this because they have earlier copies of the manuscript and this passage is not in any of them. It had to have been added by a scribe who might have had the best intentions, but nonetheless, changed the text to include something that wasn't in the original. Some Bibles have a footnote to this passage explaining that it is an addition to the original manuscript. But most people don't read footnotes, do they?

The next example concerns Holy Communion. It's toward the end of the Gospel where Jesus is having his last supper with the disciples. Most of us, at one time or another, have heard the words spoken by a clergy member during Holy Communion. We often hear how on the night he was betrayed, Jesus took a loaf of bread, gave thanks, and then broke it, saying it was his body which was given for you, and to do it (partake of it) in his memory. Then, after supper, Jesus took the cup of wine, and again gave thanks, saying it was his blood in the new covenant which is shed for the remission of sins.

Of course, this isn't exactly what's recited in churches. Each denomination has its own Words of Institution, as they are called. What's important to see here is how Jesus took bread, gave thanks, broke it, and then shared it with his disciples. Then, after supper, he took a cup of wine, gave thanks, and then shared it with his disciples.

However, in the twenty-second chapter of Luke's Gospel, we read of the events in a different order – Jesus first takes the cup of wine and tells his disciples to divide it among themselves, saying he will not drink of the fruit of the vine until the Kingdom of God comes. Then, he takes a loaf of bread, gives thanks, breaks it, and gives it to his disciples, saying it is his body which is given for them, and to remember him whenever they do it. So it sounds like the writer of Luke's Gospel just got things turned around; he just switched the order, right? That could be the answer until we read the very next verse.

The very next verse in that passage, the verse following Jesus sharing the loaf of bread, is this:

> "And he did the same with the cup after supper, saying, 'This cup that is poured out for you is the new covenant in my blood.'" [Luke 22:20]

This verse doesn't seem to fit, does it? It wasn't in the oldest manuscripts of Luke's Gospel. It did not show up in manuscripts until after the oldest manuscripts of Luke's Gospel were in circulation. Biblical scholars believe this verse was added by a scribe to clarify that Jesus had blood – just like every other human. It also doesn't fit in with the two previous Gospels – Mark's and Matthew's – as to the order of what Jesus did first. I'm going to talk more about another addition to Luke's Gospel later – one that scholars believe was added to show Jesus was indeed a human and not a ghost.

The last example is in one of the letters toward the end of the New Testament. It occurs in the letter called First John and is referred to as the *Johannine Comma*. It's not a comma like you would write in a sentence; it's an addition to the verses in the fifth chapter of the letter. The original letter did not have the words in question. They were added hundreds of years after the letter was first written to confirm the biblical authority of the Holy Trinity, to confirm that Jesus is the Son of God and that Jesus and God are one.

I'd like to discuss the Trinity later, so I'm just going to explain the words that were added. The original text in First John reads:

> "For there are three that bear record, the Spirit, the Water, and the Blood, and these three agree in one." [1 John 5:8]

The changed text, with the additional words italicized, reads like this:

> "For there are three that bear record *in heaven, the Father, the Word, and the Holy Spirit: and these three are one. And there are three that bear witness in earth*, the Spirit, the Water, and the Blood, and these three agree in one." [1 John 5:7-8]

As you can see, the additional words change the entire context of the passage. The changed text identifies the Trinity: the Father, the Word (Jesus), and the Holy Spirit. If you were to read this passage in most Bible versions, there is a footnote explaining that it wasn't in earlier manuscripts, and some Bible versions omit the footnote completely. Again, I'd like to cover the Trinity later, if that's okay?

Defense:

That would be fine. To summarize this part of your testimony: Not only did scribes accidentally change the manuscripts, they also appear to have purposely changed them to make them read the way a scribe thought they should read – is that correct?

Doubt:

That's the way it appears. Obviously, we can't go back in time and interview the scribes, so we can't say with absolute certainty that they made the changes deliberately and for what they believed were good reasons. We can only say that the most plausible reason for the changes appears to be that the scribes

wanted the texts to be congruent with their understanding of Jesus and what he taught. There were also times when scribes appear to have deleted words because they thought the words were mistakes or they believed the deletions were necessary to portray Jesus

> *The most plausible reason for the changes appears to be that the scribes wanted the texts to be congruent with their understanding of Jesus and what he taught.*

the way the original writer wanted it to appear. They deleted the words and replaced them with other words. For example, in Mark's Gospel (the first Gospel that was written), we read in the first chapter:

> "As it is written in the prophet Isaiah, 'See, I am sending my messenger ahead of you, who will prepare your way; the voice of the one crying out in the wilderness: Prepare the way of the Lord, make his paths straight.'" [Mark 1:2-3]

This is how it was written in the earliest manuscripts. There was a problem, however, that the scribes picked up on: This quote isn't from the prophet Isaiah, it's from the prophet Malachi. The scribes took care of this misquote from the writer of Mark's Gospel by changing later manuscripts to read: "As it is written in the prophets." Instead of attributing this quote to Isaiah, medieval scribes deleted the mistaken quote and wrote, simply, "the prophets." There, problem solved.

Another change is in the second chapter of Luke's Gospel. There we read how Jesus, as a young boy, was accidentally left behind in Jerusalem when his parents went to a festival there. Their caravan was heading back home when they realized they left twelve-year-old Jesus in Jerusalem. After three days, his mother, Mary, finds him in the Temple. Mary is obviously upset, and she says to Jesus, "Child, why have you treated us like this? Look, your father and I have been searching for you in great anxiety." Jesus replies that he was in his Father's house, and she should have known that.

Scholars believe that when the scribes were reading this, they had a problem: Joseph wasn't Jesus' father. By the time this manuscript was being copied, the idea that Jesus was God's son was widely accepted as the truth. Scribes then deleted "father" in some manuscripts and replaced it with, "Your parents have been searching for you" or "Joseph and I have been searching for you." This is one example where scribes wanted to be true to the *current* understanding of who Jesus was. At that time, Jesus was believed to be the Son of God, so they changed the text to remove any doubt who his father was, and who his father wasn't.

Defense:

You're saying these are just a few examples. Can we assume there are more changes scribes made, but in the interest of time, you're explaining just these few that you've testified about?

Doubt:

That's right. There are a lot more changes made by the scribes, both accidentally and what appears to be intentionally, but I'm afraid we'd be here until tomorrow going over all of them.

Defense:

Are these changes in the manuscripts – changes made by scribes – taught in the same universities and seminaries that you've mentioned before? In other words, would people who've graduated from theological schools and clergy members who've attended seminary know about these?

Doubt:

Yes, they would. Again, only the fundamental institutions gloss over the errors in the manuscripts. And when they do teach them, it is usually from a theological point of view. The typical theological argument against them – defending the ancient texts as the authoritative word of God – is discussed, so the students can squash any of my presence later if the topic comes up.

Defense:

You just used a term that I'm sure some of the members of the jury have heard before. You said some people defend the ancient sacred texts, the manuscripts of the books of the Bible, as "the authoritative word of God." What is meant by that term?

Doubt:

Sure. There are some Christians, and folks from the other Abrahamic religions, that believe the Bible comes from God himself. They believe God inspired different men to write the Bible based on what God wanted written down. So the authority for the words in the Bible comes from God, not from man.

These same Christians sometimes add or exchange another definition of the Bible; they say the Bible is inerrant and infallible in every way. That is, it is without any errors and has no flaws in it whatsoever. That's why when the inconsistencies we have discussed so far are brought up, fundamentalist Christians are very quick to refute any such claims and defend the Bible as being a perfect book given from God.

I should add that I have no problems with anyone who believes the Bible is inerrant and infallible. As I said at the outset of this case, I have no horse in this race. I'm not trying to get someone to change their beliefs or alter their faith. I'm present to create the nudge to investigate something when it doesn't seem right, to dig a little deeper into it and see what you find. If your thoughts, opinions, and beliefs remain the same as they were before you started to ask questions, great! But to not even consider other facts – and these are facts – is to shortchange yourself. I can tell you that I know many people who have acted on me – they questioned, they investigated, they researched – and their faith became more profound because they saw the books in the Bible in a new light. Their questions actually brought them into a closer relationship with God than before they were asked.

> *Because of Doubt, many people have questioned, investigated, and researched the Bible – and their faith became more profound. Their questions actually brought them into a closer relationship with God.*

I might also add that the fundamentalist Christians have the most problems with me. They, and their churches, would rather see me annihilated than be a presence in their lives or in their houses of worship. For them, I think I'm seen as the enemy, as a danger for the spiritual well-being of all concerned. I hold nothing against them for having that view of me; as someone much wiser than me once said, "It is what it is."

Defense:

Thank you for explaining that for the members of the jury. Let's move on.

When you began your testimony about the Bible, you mentioned contradictions in some books. Can you elaborate on them for the jury?

Doubt:

When I said there are contradictions, I was referring to passages from different books that are telling the same story of an event or quotes that are at odds with one another. These are parts of the text where one book tells a story and another book contradicts the events in the same story.

I gave the example of the creation stories in the Book of Genesis at the beginning of this trial. I hope I showed how the stories of the same event, the creation of the earth, contradicted each other in the two chapters. There are many more examples of this kind of contradiction in the New Testament.

It's probably best to start off slow before going deeper into some of the more controversial, and in my view, unexplainable contradictions in the books of the Bible. Here's a question: Who was Jesus' grandfather on his dad's side of the family; that is, what was the name of Joseph's father? That sounds like a simple question, doesn't it? All of us have a father who had a father; we all have had only one father, and he had only one father. And when I say father, I'm talking about our biological father – our bloodline, our genealogy as it were.

There are two books in the New Testament that describe the birth of Jesus: the Gospels of Matthew and Luke. Matthew's Gospel traces the bloodline of Jesus back to Abraham, and Luke's Gospel traces it all the way back to Adam, as in Adam and Eve – the first two people on earth.

Even if we take out the implausibility of being able to trace one's ancestry back thousands of years, we can be pretty sure we have an accurate identification of at least the grandfather of Jesus, and maybe even his great-grandfather, right? Unfortunately, the books of the Bible that document Jesus' grandfather and great-great-grandfather disagree on who they were. In Matthew, he is Jacob, the son of Matthan, who was the son of Eleazar; in Luke, Joseph is the son of Heli, who was the son of Matthat.

The two books that trace the bloodline of Jesus can't go back three generations without being at odds with each other. There are other discrepancies in these genealogies, but just using common sense, is it even possible to trace someone's bloodline back as far as it is recorded in the Gospels of Matthew and Luke? There were no birth certificates back then, no computerized cataloging of birth information, no Internet to conduct searches on; all they had were oral traditions that were handed down through the generations. And yet, there are still those who claim the Bible is the inerrant and infallible word of God. These facts alone, before going any further into the Gospels, should bring me into the discussion. Instead, any mention of me brings disdain, and occasionally, some rather interesting explanations. But I'm not here to discuss anyone's explanations or rationalizations, am I?

Defense:

No, *Doubt*, you're not. Let's move forward into the Gospels.

Doubt:

Okay. But as soon as we get to the birth stories of Jesus, we once again run into contradictions.

Defense:

What do you mean?

Doubt:

As I said, two of the four canonical Gospels, that is, the Gospels in the New Testament, narrate the birth of Jesus, sometimes called the *infancy narratives*. While there are many differences between the two accounts, there are contradictions that appear to be difficult, at best, to reconcile. I'm going to stick with just the contradictions.

In Matthew's Gospel, the first recorded account, we read that Joseph and Mary were in Bethlehem when Mary got pregnant. Joseph wanted to leave her because they hadn't had sexual relations, but an angel of the Lord appeared to him in a dream telling him that Mary was made pregnant by the Holy Spirit to fulfill what was told by the prophets – that a virgin shall give birth to the Messiah.

King Herod heard about the birth of the "King of the Jews" from the wise men who came looking for the baby Jesus. Herod, being a jealous king, hatched a plan to have Jesus brought to him, and asked the wise men to return to him once they located this baby Messiah. But the wise men were warned of the plan in a dream so, after visiting Jesus and his new parents in a house, they returned to their country by a different route.

When King Herod saw that he'd been tricked by the wise men, he ordered all the children under two years old in Bethlehem to be killed. This is referred to as the Slaughter of the Infants in some Bibles. Before that order was carried out, Joseph had another dream where an angel of the Lord warned him they were in danger and instructed that he take Mary and Jesus and flee to Egypt and remain there until the death of Herod. This was done to fulfill what was spoken by the prophet: "Out of Egypt I have called my son." [Matthew 2:15]

When Herod died, Joseph had yet another dream where an angel of the Lord appeared to him, telling him to return to Israel because Herod had died. Joseph packed up Mary and Jesus and headed toward Israel. But one more dream was in store for Joseph. This time, he was warned that Herod's son was ruling over Judea in place of his father, and it wasn't safe to go back. So Joseph set off to the area of Galilee and he settled his family in a small town called Nazareth. This, too, fulfilled what was told through the prophets: "He will be called a Nazorean." [Matthew 2:23]

To recap Matthew's Gospel: Joseph and Mary were living in Bethlehem when Joseph had a dream that Mary – a virgin – was pregnant by the Holy Spirit, which was foretold by the prophets. They were visited by the wise men in their home. Joseph had a dream telling him to take Jesus and Mary and flee to Egypt, which was to fulfill what was told by the prophets. After Herod died, Joseph had another dream telling him it was safe to return to Israel, but on the way there, he had another dream telling him to go to a town in Galilee and settle there, to fulfill what was told through the prophets.

The story of Jesus' birth in Luke's Gospel is quite different. Luke's birth narrative begins with Jesus and Mary already living in Nazareth, engaged to be married. Mary was visited by an angel named Gabriel who told her she will conceive in her womb and bear a child, and she shall name the child Jesus. This child will become great and will be called the Son of the Most High, and God will give him the throne of David.

Mary, being a virgin, was perplexed – how could she conceive and give birth if she was a virgin? The angel Gabriel explained how the Holy Spirit will impregnate her and when the child is born, he will be the Son of God. Fast-forwarding through a bunch of verses, we learn that the emperor sent out a decree that everyone in the world had to register for a census. Everyone had to go to the town of their ancestors to register – some Bible versions explain this as a census, others as a tax. Since Joseph was from the lineage of David, he was required to return to the city of David, called Bethlehem. So Joseph brought his expectant wife, Mary, with him to Bethlehem. While there, the time had come for Mary to give birth. But because there was no room at the inn for them, their baby was born in a manger.

An angel appeared to some shepherds who were in the fields minding their flocks. This angel told them that the Messiah, the Lord, was born in the city of David, and told them where to find this child. The shepherds went and found Jesus wrapped in bands of cloth lying in a manger. Jesus was circumcised eight days after his birth, as per the law, and then his parents presented him in the Temple. When they finished everything that was required of them by the law, they returned to Nazareth where we're told Jesus was raised and became a young man.

To recap Luke's narration: Mary and Joseph were living in Nazareth when Mary had a visit from an angel who told her she would become pregnant by the Holy Spirit. The emperor of that time called for a census or tax where everyone had to go to the town of their ancestor to register. Joseph brought his pregnant wife, Mary, with him to Bethlehem, which was known as the city of David; he went there because he was from David's bloodline. While in Bethlehem, Mary went into labor, but because the inn was full, she gave birth to Jesus and had to lay him in a manger. After the customary eight days, Jesus was circumcised according to Jewish law and then he was presented in the Temple by his parents. Joseph and Mary then returned to Nazareth where they raised Jesus.

So which account is what really happened?

Were Joseph and Mary originally from Bethlehem or Nazareth? It depends on which Gospel you read.

Who was made aware that Mary was pregnant? Was it Joseph in a dream – or Mary when she was visited by the angel Gabriel? It depends on which Gospel you read.

Was Jesus born in a house or in a manger? It depends on which Gospel you read.

Who visited Jesus – wise men from the east or shepherds from nearby fields? It depends on which Gospel you read.

After Jesus was born, did Joseph take his family to Egypt or did he return to Nazareth? It depends on which Gospel you read.

These are details that stand in contrast to each other if you place each narrative side by side and look at them. And these are just the contradictions between the birth narratives themselves.

Defense:

Is that to imply that there are other types of contradictions in these stories?

Doubt:

Yes, contradictions with what is historically known. In each narrative, there is a problem with what is told as having happened with what has been recorded as history. Or, to be precise, what has never been recorded as history.

Defense:

Can you explain for the jury what you mean by that?

Doubt:

The authors of both Gospels are tasked with telling how Jesus would need to be born in Bethlehem. This is to satisfy what the prophet Micah had said six hundred years earlier:

> "But you, O Bethlehem of Ephrathah, who are one of the little clans of Judah, from you shall come forth for me one who is to rule Israel, whose origin is from old, from ancient days." [Micah 5:2]

So each author had to make sure Jesus was born in Bethlehem.

For the author of Matthew's Gospel, this was easy – Joseph and Mary were already living in Bethlehem, and Mary gave birth to Jesus in a house there. However, the author repeatedly points out how certain things were done and said to fulfill the prophets – presumably to confirm and prove what was said by ancient prophets quoted in the Old Testament. If you recall from the birth narrative, we are told no less than three times that something was done to fulfill the prophets.

The way the author gets Jesus to Egypt – in order to fulfill the prophecy that God's son would be called out of Egypt – is to share the story of King Herod killing every newborn in Bethlehem. Biblical scholars, historians, and anthropologists have searched all the ancient Jewish and Roman empire artifacts and books known to have existed at that time, and *there is no evidence to support the story that the king had every child under the age of two killed.* Certainly, if this had occurred, someone, somewhere would have written about it as there were historians of that day doing credible work in that part of the world. Simply put, this story of children being killed contradicts what history tells us.

Moving on to Luke's Gospel and the story of the census: Luke's author has the task of getting Mary and Joseph into Bethlehem so Jesus can be born there – to fulfill the prophet Micah. In Luke, Joseph and Mary are required to go to Bethlehem to register for the census or the tax – depending on which source you read. Since Joseph was from the bloodline of David, he was required to go to the town where David lived and register there.

First, as with the story of the Slaughter of the Infants, scholars, historians, and anthropologists can find no record – no evidence – that the emperor at that time, Augustus, called for a census or an empire-wide tax, let alone a census or tax where the entire world was required to register! Nothing recorded by ancient Jewish or Roman historians give even a hint that a census was taken then or that a special tax was levied, let alone one where everyone had to go back to their place of origin.

Think about it for a minute and just logically consider a few things: According to the lineage as recorded in the Gospels, there were fourteen generations between Jesus and David. In that time, that would have been around five hundred years. Would any of you, the members of the jury, using all the technology we have available to us today, be able to trace your father's ancestry back fourteen generations? Would you be able to figure out where that side of your family lived five hundred years ago?

Even with websites devoted to ancestries, the most any of us go back is four or five generations. Fourteen generations? In a time when there were no birth records kept, no registrar of records in each town, and no sophisticated means of communication or documentation, the likelihood of the possibility of this happening is nil. And then consider the logistics of getting everyone to their respective towns. It's estimated that at the time of Jesus' birth, the city of Bethlehem had about three hundred people living in it. If everyone who came from the lineage of David, every descendant from the fourteen generations, there would be tens and tens of thousands of people in Bethlehem to be registered for the census. A town that size could never have held such a large number. As with the story of the Slaughter of the Infants, there is nothing historically evident to support it and it is implausible to have been possible at best.

Defense:

That certainly makes sense when you explain it like that. If this concludes your testimony about the contradictions in the birth narratives, we can move on.

The Court:

Counselor, it's getting near lunchtime and this is probably a good time for a recess. It will give the jury a chance to digest not just their lunch, but everything *Doubt* has testified to so far.

Defense:

We have no objections to that, Your Honor!

The Court:

Okay, then. We'll take our lunchbreak now, and when we return, we will continue with the testimony of *Doubt.*

Chapter 5:

Early Afternoon Testimony

*Contradictions in Jesus' Ministry * Gospel Contradictions * Gospel Writers'*
*Agendas * Contradictions in Jesus' Death and Resurrection * Heaven and Hell*
and the Kingdom of God

The Court:

Welcome back, ladies and gentlemen of the jury. I hope you
had a chance to take a break and consider the testimony so far,
and hopefully you grabbed a bite to eat or you enjoyed a
beverage of your liking.

Counselor, if you're ready, you can continue with your
examination of *Doubt.*

Defense:

Thank you, Judge.

Doubt, let's move on to other parts of the Gospels. What
contradictions are there in the ministry of Jesus and his arrest,
crucifixion, and resurrection?

Doubt:

In the interest of time, I'd like to bring up just one contradiction in the ministry of Jesus, and then go to the end of the Gospels, if that's all right? There are contradictions, to be sure, when the same stories in the four Gospels are compared to one another. But most of them are minor in detail when compared to the contradictions at the end of the Gospels – at the end of Jesus' life. And if we were to go through every contradiction or discrepancy, we'd all be bored out of our minds. So I'd like to point out just the contradictions in what's documented in his ministry, and then move on to Jesus' death and resurrection.

Defense:

What is the contradiction in Jesus' ministry that you would like to explain?

Doubt:

The contradiction I'm going to discuss isn't one where two books of the Bible disagree on the same event; instead, this is a contradiction where Jesus seems to disagree with – well, Jesus disagrees with Jesus and with the apostle Paul. What Jesus says in one Gospel seems to contradict what he says in another Gospel, and it definitely contradicts what Paul says. Let me explain.

If you ask most people, they would probably tell you they've heard the belief that unless you believe in Jesus and accept him as your Lord and Savior, you won't go to Heaven. Put another way, the only way to get to Heaven is to believe in Jesus. Some would say that one is saved if they believe in Jesus. I guess that's where all those "Jesus Saves" bumper stickers come from.

I don't think you need to be a Christian to appreciate this theology. There's nothing a person must do down here on earth to gain access to Heaven other than just believe in Jesus – no special offerings, no sacrifices, no good deeds. Just believe in Jesus and your reservation in Heaven is confirmed.

This belief is grounded in a couple of passages from John's Gospel. The first is a very well-known passage that's shared at many Christian funerals. It begins in the fourteenth chapter on the night Jesus was going to be arrested. Jesus had just finished the last meal he would eat with the disciples while he was alive. He told his disciples that they shouldn't let their hearts be troubled, he was going ahead of them to his father to prepare a place for them and he would one day return for them and bring them to his father. Thomas asked him, "Lord, we do not know where you are going. How can we know the way?" Jesus replies, "I am the way, the truth, and the light. No one comes to the Father except through me."

Another passage is from the sixth chapter. Jesus says: "Very truly I tell you, whoever believes has eternal life. I am the bread of life. Your ancestors ate the manna in the wilderness, and they died. This is the bread that comes down from Heaven, so that one may eat of it and not die. I am the living bread that came down from Heaven. Whoever eats of this bread will live forever; and the bread that I will give for the life of the world is my flesh."

The final passage I want to mention from John's Gospel is one that very few people can deny hearing or seeing it on billboards along the highways and on posters at football games. It's from the third chapter: "For God so loved the world that he gave his only Son, so that everyone who believes in him may not perish but have eternal life." Even if you don't know the words, you've read the signs: John 3:16.

In my first example, Jesus seems to be saying that no one gets into Heaven, goes to God, except through him. In the second, Jesus is saying if you believe, you will have eternal life; for he is the bread of life and whoever takes in that bread will live forever. When these statements are added to Jesus explicitly saying that anyone who believes in him will gain eternal life, it's easy to see how some people interpret them to mean unless you believe in Jesus, you're not going to Heaven.

The apostle Paul spells it out in some of his letters: The only way a person can be justified (that is, right with God) is to believe in Jesus. Paul says that keeping the law, doing good deeds, and making sacrifices can't get you into Heaven – you can't earn your way into Heaven. The only way to be saved from eternal damnation in a fiery realm is to believe in Jesus. Once you do that, you're set.

Now, let's look at a passage from Matthew's Gospel. It's a passage in the twenty-fifth chapter, referred to as the Judgment of the Nations. Here Jesus says that when the Son of man comes in his glory, he will separate people from one another just like a shepherd separates the sheep from the goats: The sheep will be at his right hand – the side of honor – and the goats will be at his left. He says the ones on his right are blessed and they will inherit the Kingdom of Heaven. This is because when he was hungry, they gave him food; when he was thirsty, they gave him something to drink; when he was a stranger, they welcomed him; when he was naked, they clothed him; when he was sick, they took care of him; and when he was in prison, they visited him.

The righteous ones – the ones on his right-hand side – ask, "Lord, when was it that we saw you hungry and gave you food, or thirsty and gave you something to drink? And when was it that we saw you a stranger and welcomed you, or naked and gave you clothing? And when was it that we saw you sick or in prison and visited you?" The King answers them: "Truly I tell you, just as you did it to one of the least of these who are members of my family, you did it to me."

He then looks to the ones on his left and tells them they are going to spend eternity in fire prepared for the devil and his angels. He tells them he was hungry and they did not feed him; he was thirsty and they gave him nothing to drink; he was a stranger and they did not welcome him; he was naked and they did not clothe him; he was sick and in prison and they did not visit him. Those people ask how that can be? They never saw him hungry or thirsty or a stranger or naked or sick or in prison. The King replies that whatever they did not do for the least of these, they did not do it for him. So they will go away to eternal punishment, but the righteous ones will get eternal life.

When you look at the three passages I shared from John's Gospel and then add what Paul says in his letters, there is no doubt that you can't earn your way into Heaven – you can't do good deeds to gain eternal life. The only way to have eternal life in Heaven with God is to believe in Jesus. Period.

But when you read the Judgment of the Nations, Jesus is explicit when he says those who do good deeds are the ones who will have eternal life in Heaven with God. Jesus gives examples of that to make his point clear. What's more striking is that the righteous ones say they don't even know the King, they've never met the Lord.

> *Is it faith – belief in Jesus – that gets you a place in Heaven? Or, is it doing good deeds here on earth, taking care of the least in our communities? It all depends on which books you read.*

All they know is they did good works for people in need. These people, for all we know, never heard of Jesus; it certainly looks that way by the way the passage reads.

So here is a contradiction of Jesus' own words, as well as a contradiction between the apostle Paul's teachings and the teachings of Jesus. Is it faith – belief in Jesus – that gets you a place in Heaven? Or is it doing good deeds here on earth, taking care of the least in our communities? It all depends on which books you read. And so, we have more confusion because of another contradiction.

Defense:

I have to wonder what the members of the jury make of this. I wonder if they are as confused as I am about how to gain eternal life. It certainly gives one a reason to stop and wonder, doesn't it?

Let's move on to the death and resurrection of Jesus. You said there were some contradictions in that part of the Gospels as well?

Doubt:

Let me start by saying I think the narratives of the arrest and Crucifixion of Jesus are some of the most heart-wrenching and moving stories I've ever read. And when I say stories, I'm not suggesting that the Crucifixion of Jesus is made up. There is at least one historical source outside the Bible, a Jewish historian named Josephus, who documented the Crucifixion of Jesus. Most biblical scholars and historians believe that Jesus was in fact put on trial for insurrection and put to death by the most agonizing and humiliating means the Romans had at their disposal – crucifixion.

When I say there are contradictions in the narratives, I'm not suggesting these discrepancies point to Jesus not being crucified. I'm saying there are contradictions in the descriptions of how the events unfolded. Three of the Gospels each describe a very specific event, but they describe it differently. The discrepancies are so subtle that most people look right past them. But I think the contradictions are significant because it appears the writer of each Gospel was trying to offer a symbolism about the event I'm going to talk about.

The Gospels of Mark, Matthew, and Luke all have an almost identical story line – they have most of the same stories in them, and they are similar in the order they happened in the life of Jesus. Because they are so similar, they are called the synoptic Gospels. The word *synoptic* comes from a Greek word roughly meaning to have the same view, or "seen together."

By the way, I'm not sure if I said this before: The word *Gospel* is also a Greek word; it means good news. So the Gospels tell the good news of Jesus. I thought you might find that interesting.

Anyway, the subtle discrepancies that I find interesting are the passages right when Jesus dies. No, I'm not a sadist who enjoys watching another human being die. I find these passages interesting because of the symbolism they offer in each account. I'm talking about the curtain in the Temple when Jesus dies. The three synoptic Gospels all record it tearing in two when Jesus dies. But the subtle difference in exactly when the curtain is torn is what I find compelling.

The Temple curtain enclosed the innermost part of the Temple. It separated the Holy of Holies, and inside this inner sanctum is where God resided. No one was permitted inside this part of the Temple except for the high priest, and then only once a year to offer sacrifices and prayers to God. In essence, the Temple curtain separated God from everyone else. The high priest acted as a liaison between the people and God when he visited this innermost part of the Temple once a year. This part of the Temple was the most sacred of sacred places in the Temple.

I'm going to go in the reverse order of when the curtain was torn. In Mark's Gospel, we are told that Jesus had been on the cross for about six hours when he cried out, "My God, my God, why have you forsaken me?" Very shortly after that, Jesus gave out a loud cry and died. Then, the curtain of the Temple was torn in two, from top to bottom. [Mark 15:33-38]

Matthew's Gospel also says that Jesus had been on the cross until three o'clock in the afternoon when he cries out, "My God, my God, why have you forsaken me?" Just as in Mark, very shortly after that, Jesus cried out again and breathed his last. *At that very same time*, the curtain of the Temple was torn in two, from top to bottom. [Matthew 27:45-51]

Luke's account, just like in Mark and Matthew, says Jesus was on the cross and it was about three in the afternoon. But Luke's Gospel says the curtain of the Temple was torn in two *before* Jesus died. Then, Jesus cried out in a loud voice, "Father, into your hands I commend my spirit." Jesus then died after saying that. [Luke 23:44-46]

If you were to read each of the synoptic Gospels, you might think they were the same. But a careful reading of each Gospel shows discrepancies in the details of when the curtain tears.

Now that you've looked at these narratives in depth, when did the Temple curtain tear in two?

The writer of Mark's Gospel says the curtain was torn right *after* Jesus breathed his last breath. The writer of Matthew's Gospel says the curtain was torn *at the same time* Jesus breathed his last breath. But the writer of Luke's Gospel says the curtain was torn just *before* Jesus died. A curtain can only be torn in two one time – so all three accounts can't be historically accurate. Either Mark is right, and Matthew and Luke are wrong; Matthew is right, and Mark and Luke are wrong; or Luke is right, and Mark and Matthew are wrong.

While it is possible that all three writers got it wrong, it is impossible that all three got it right. So here is a very subtle contradiction that most people would never consider unless they placed the synoptic Gospels side by side and compared each passage. This is what biblical scholars and historians do, and they are the ones who've found all the contradictions and discrepancies I've talked about so far, as well as all the rest I'll be talking about.

I want the members of the jury to know that none of what I've testified to so far, and nothing I will testify to for the remainder of this trial, was discovered by me. I just happen to enjoy researching this stuff, and in that research, I've read a lot of books from many wonderful scholars, historians, and theologians; they are the ones who deserve all the credit for their academic commitment to the Bible.

That being said, I'd like to take the contradictions I just mentioned one step further. This has nothing to do with any discrepancies, it's just something scholars have discussed and debated, and I'm sure they will continue to discuss and debate for years to come.

Can I go off on just a short tangent, Your Honor?

The Court:

As long as you keep it short!

Doubt:

I will, Judge, I promise. I certainly don't want to piss off anyone at this point in the trial.

Oh, crap; I said piss again. Sorry, Your Honor – old habits die hard.

The Court:

Will you get on with it!

Doubt:

I'm sorry, Your Honor. I'm moving forward.

Here's the thing: Biblical scholars and theologians have been discussing why the writers would have the curtain tear at the time they say it did. Although its location is not exactly known today, the site where Jesus was crucified was not within sight distance of the inner part of the Temple in Jerusalem. And there is no indication that there were any witnesses in the area of the Temple when Jesus was crucified. Many scholars and historians believe the writers of the Gospels may have taken some artistic and historic license in recording the tearing of the Temple curtain. That doesn't mean it didn't happen, it just means I've shown up in many of those discussions.

The arguments for the three different accounts of when exactly the curtain was torn in two center around the symbolism of the tearing itself. The tearing of the curtain represented the removal of any separation between the people and God. Once the curtain was torn in two, there was no longer anything between the people and their God. But – what was it that caused that liberation?

In Mark's Gospel, the curtain is torn right after Jesus dies; does this mean it was Jesus' death that removed any barriers between God and his people? In Matthew's Gospel, the curtain is torn at the same time Jesus dies; does this mean that the act of dying removed the barriers? In Luke's Gospel, the curtain is torn while Jesus was still alive, as he was suffering just before he died; is it the suffering of Jesus that removes any barriers between us and God?

These are the questions theologians have debated, and I'm sure will continue to debate for years. Some people, and some churches, base part of their theology on the death, the dying, or the suffering of Jesus. And once again, I find myself getting dragged into the discussions and debates.

Defense:

It certainly sounds like the writers of each Gospel had their own agenda and for at least three of them, the tearing of the Temple curtain shows that they were each trying to convey something to the readers.

Doubt:

We've got to remember that the writers of the Gospels lived after the death of Jesus, in a different part of the empire, and with a different lifestyle. These were men who were writing anywhere from forty to seventy years after the death of Jesus – in a language Jesus never spoke, and from a social and financial background completely different than his. What these writers of the Gospel were trying to do is explain who Jesus was and what his ministry was all about. No one questions their intentions and I think we owe it to them to give them the benefit of assuming they were doing the best they could in recounting the life and ministry of Jesus.

We also have to accept the fact that these were Jewish men writing in a Jewish community with social norms that were foreign – quite literally – to the people who would later look at the manuscripts and determine what became canon and what didn't. Remember, Jesus was a Jew and he taught from a Jewish perspective to Jewish people about Jewish law. After his death, his message was shared in synagogues by people who were his followers. These people were sharing the lessons he taught and the manner in which he lived. As time went on, his message and teachings spread outside the walls of the synagogues; that is to say, non-Jews were beginning to hear about him. As Christianity built up steam over the decades after his death, it spread faster in the gentile communities than in the Jewish communities. Pagans, as they were called in ancient Rome, were converting to Christianity faster than Jews were. And by the end of the first century, Christianity had moved away from the Jewish traditions to become more than just an offshoot of some Jewish sect; Christianity had become its own religion.

The problem is that it was now being taught by non-Jews who lived outside the area of the empire where it began. People – all men of course, with no background in Judaism and with no idea of the accepted Jewish traditions and understandings – took control of Christianity and the sacred texts that were written about it. With no understanding of Judaism, the earliest of the Church fathers began interpreting what was written in the Gospels and the letters from Paul through their non-Jewish lenses. And with that, they took everything that was written down in the books that eventually became the New Testament as being 100 percent true and factual. They had no idea of the Jewish Midrashic teachings, nor the oral traditions that were used to continue and explain different theological concepts of their time.

The point is that Jewish texts, written by Jewish men, in Jewish communities, for a Jewish audience, were taken over by people who had no idea of the traditions, social norms, and theological ideas of them. So unless we were raised in a Jewish household and learned the Jewish laws and traditions, we, too, are reading ancient sacred texts through lenses that the texts weren't meant to be interpreted through. That's why I said we should probably give the writers of the Gospels the benefit of assuming they were doing the best they could.

Defense:

I can honestly say that I never thought about the Bible and the beginning of Christianity that way before just now. It starts to make sense when you consider it that way.

But we have to keep moving on with the contradictions in the New Testament. Are there any other contradictions about the death of Jesus in the Gospels?

Doubt:

Yes, both his death and resurrection.

After Jesus died, we are told he was buried in a tomb; all four Gospels state this. The contradictions arise when we look at who visited the tomb after he was buried and what they found when they got there. As we will see, different Gospels tell different stories.

The first Gospel to be written was Mark, and according to the writer of Mark, the tomb was visited by Mary Magdalene; Mary, the mother of James; and Salome, a disciple of Jesus. When they got there, they saw that the stone that was put in front of the tomb had been moved away. They saw a young man dressed in a white robe who told them Jesus had been raised. He instructed them to go tell the disciples that Jesus is in Galilee and he will meet them there. The women fled from the tomb and said nothing to anyone because they were afraid. [Mark 16:1-8]

Matthew's Gospel says the tomb was visited by Mary Magdalene and the other Mary. When they got to the tomb, there was a great earthquake and an angel of the Lord descended from Heaven and rolled back the stone and sat on it. He told the women that Jesus had been raised and they should go quickly and tell the disciples that Jesus was going ahead of them to Galilee where they will see him. They left the tomb quickly and as they were running to tell the disciples, Jesus appeared to them. Jesus told them to tell his disciples to go to Galilee where they will see him. [Matthew 28:1-10]

Luke's Gospel records the event this way: Mary Magdalene, Joanna, Mary the mother of James, and the women who had come with Jesus from Galilee went to the tomb and when they got there, the stone was rolled away. They went into the tomb and saw that Jesus' body wasn't there. Suddenly, two men in dazzling clothes stood beside them and told them to remember that Jesus told them he would be resurrected on the third day. The women went and told the disciples, but they didn't believe the women. Peter ran to the tomb, went inside, and saw only the linen cloths that Jesus was buried in. [Luke 24:1-12]

Finally, John's Gospel says Mary Magdalene went to the tomb alone and saw that the stone had been rolled away. She ran and told two disciples who then ran to the tomb to see for themselves. When they got there, they went into the tomb and saw only the linens Jesus was buried in. They didn't understand what was happening, and they returned to their homes. Mary stayed at the tomb crying. As she was crying, she looked into the tomb and saw two angels sitting where Jesus' body had been laid. After a brief conversation, she looked around and saw Jesus standing there, but she did not recognize him, she thought he might be a gardener. He asked her why she was weeping, and she replied it was because she thought his body had been removed. Jesus called her by name, and it was then that she recognized him as Jesus. He told her to go tell his disciples that he is ascending to his father, and Mary went and told his disciples. [John 20:1-18]

If one was to place these four narratives next to one another, they would immediately see not only the differences, but the contradictions as well. The contradictions include which women and how many went to the tomb, what did they see when they got there, what were they told to do, and what did they do.

The final contradiction I want to bring up is the question of how many days Jesus spent with his disciples after the Resurrection. The Book of Acts is believed to be written by the same person who wrote Luke's Gospel. This book describes the acts of the apostles after Jesus' death, and how they began to spread his message. The Book of Acts says Jesus was with his disciples for forty days after the Resurrection before he was taken up to Heaven. But in the Gospel of Luke, we're told Jesus ascended to Heaven early the same evening of his resurrection. The Gospel of Mark also says Jesus ascended to Heaven the same day as his resurrection.

What's interesting here is not so much that the account in Mark's Gospel differs from the Book of Acts – it's that Luke's Gospel and the Book of Acts differ! Both the Gospel of Luke and the Book of Acts are believed to have been written in the same decade within years of each other, which was about fifty-five to sixty years after the Resurrection. One wonders if the same writer of both books was confused, forgot, or intentionally gave two different accounts. It's definitely an interesting observation, don't you think?

Defense:

Interesting, and maybe even a little confusing.

Doubt:

Hey, welcome to my world!

The contradictions regarding Jesus' death come from what his demeanor and final words were. If you were to lay the Gospels out next to each other in the order they were written – Mark, Matthew, Luke, then John – you would see a change in Jesus' demeanor from one of anguish and despair to forgiveness and acceptance.

In Mark's Gospel, we're told that before his arrest he was greatly distressed and agitated, and told his disciples that he was deeply grieved. Matthew's Gospel tells the same account. Luke's Gospel says he was in anguish, but an angel of the Lord appeared and gave him strength. In all three of these Gospels, Jesus prays to the Father that he might "remove this cup (of suffering)" or "let this cup pass from me" if it was God's will.

By the time we get to John's Gospel, Jesus is praying to the Father for his disciples' protection prior to his arrest. There is no mention, or any indication, that Jesus was anything other than calm and loving toward his disciples. And notice how his prayer is completely different than the three previous Gospels: In the synoptic Gospels, Jesus is praying for himself; in John's Gospel, he is praying for his disciples.

The other differences in the Gospels are the last words Jesus spoke while on the cross. The first two Gospels, Mark and Matthew, say Jesus cried out, "My God, my God, why have you forsaken me?" [Mark 15:34, Matthew 27:46] Luke's Gospel says that as Jesus was being crucified, he prayed, "Father, forgive them; for they do not know what they are doing." [Luke 23:34] It then records a conversation between Jesus and a criminal who was being crucified next to him. The criminal asks Jesus to remember him when he comes into his kingdom. Jesus replies to the criminal, "Truly I tell you, today you will be with me in Paradise." Jesus' final last words follow: "Father, into your hands I commend my spirit." [Luke 23:39-43]

John's Gospel has Jesus talking with women, including his mother, who had gathered at the foot of the cross. After a brief conversation, Jesus says, "I am thirsty." Then, after taking a sip from a sponge that was lifted up to him on a branch, Jesus' last words were, "It is finished." [John 19:26-30]

As you can see, Mark's Gospel and Matthew's Gospel are pretty much the same, but Luke portrays Jesus in a different way: He doesn't ask God why God abandoned him, and he even asks God to forgive those who are putting him to death. John's Gospel has Jesus talking with his mother, then saying it is finished.

There are those who argue that just because one line from what Jesus said in one Gospel isn't documented in another Gospel doesn't mean he didn't say it. In fact, on Good Friday, church services all over the world include *The Sayings of Jesus*, also called *The Seven Last Words from the Cross*, in their liturgy. These all come from taking what was said in the Gospels of Mark and Matthew, then adding the words from Luke's Gospel and the words from John's Gospel. If one were to read just one of the Gospels, they wouldn't come away with seven last words; it's only when the four Gospels are combined that we get the seven last words (which are a combination of sayings attributed to Christ on the cross, and total more than seven actual words).

My point here isn't to say that there is no way Jesus said all those words from the cross, commonly called the Seven Last Words; he most certainly could have. Instead, it's to show that for whatever reason, each Gospel writer either chose to purposely omit what was said in the other Gospels, or that writer didn't hear of them when he was writing his Gospel. In any case, along with Jesus' attitude, the differences are significant enough that they contradict each other in both Jesus' words and demeanor.

Defense:

I guess that does it for the contradictions in the New Testament, right?

Doubt:

No, but we'd be here all day if we went over every one of them. Like the story of Jesus raising a girl from the dead: In one Gospel, we're told her father, a leader in the synagogue, asks Jesus to come heal her because she is very sick, but on the way to his house, Jesus learns she has died before he can get there in time. Jesus goes to the house anyway, and he goes inside and raises her from the dead. In another Gospel, the same story is told, but in that version of the story, the girl's father tells Jesus that his daughter has died and asks Jesus if he can raise her from the dead.

And there's the story of Jesus cleansing the Temple – the story of the angry Jesus flipping over the tables in the Temple. In the synoptic Gospels, Jesus does this at the end of his ministry. When he enters Jerusalem for the Passover, he goes to the Temple and sees what's going on and becomes upset. That sets up the arrest of Jesus and, ultimately, his crucifixion on the cross. In John's Gospel, however, this event takes place at the beginning of Jesus' ministry. John's Gospel has three Passovers, meaning that book covered three years of Jesus' ministry – one Passover per year. We're told in John's Gospel that this incident occurred during the first Passover, so it happened at the beginning of Jesus' three-year ministry.

And then there are the stories of—

Defense:

Hold on. Hold on, *Doubt*. Why don't we stop where we are with the contradictions and move on to other reasons you enter the religious and faith pictures?

Doubt:

Sorry. Sometimes I get carried away.

Okay, what's next on your list of questions for me?

Defense:

Since we just finished talking about the Resurrection of Jesus, why don't we move on to Heaven and hell. Surely, the Bible is clear about these two places.

Doubt:

You might want to buckle your seatbelts.

Defense:

Seriously? I mean, come on. Everyone knows Jesus went to Heaven. And when they die, his believers go there to be with him for eternity. It's right there in the Bible – isn't it?

Doubt:

> Of course, it is. It's just that Jesus never taught it, and neither Heaven nor hell are mentioned in the Old Testament.

Defense:

> Oh, so it is there. Wait. What? What do you mean Jesus never taught it and Heaven and hell aren't in the Old Testament?

Doubt:

> This is going to take a little bit of a setup and some background. Judge, I don't want to get you upset by going off on a tangent – again. Is it all right if I explain a few things to help it all make sense?

The Court:

> As long as it's germane to the question being asked of you. Just do your best to stay on track.

Doubt:

> Thanks, Judge. I don't want to piss you off. I have a feeling this is going to piss off more than a couple of people anyway. And the last thing I want to do is start off on the wrong foot with Your Honor. Have you ever done that, Judge? Ever start off on the wrong foot?

The Court:

> Defense Counsel.

Defense:

> Yes, Your Honor.

The Court:

> Would you please advise your client that his last comments would be *the definition* of a tangent? And if he doesn't get back

on track fast, I'm going to have you move on to your next question.

Defense:

Yes, Your Honor, of course.

Doubt, you have to answer just the question that is asked of you. It's important if you want to be given the latitude you asked of the Judge. Just stick with the topic. Okay?

Doubt:

Got it. Sorry, it won't happen again.

To answer your questions, Heaven – that place where our souls go when we die – and hell aren't in the Old Testament. A lot of people, it seems, have a belief that Heaven and hell are in the Old Testament and Jesus took them and explained them more fully or quantified them better than they were originally written about. The truth is, the Heaven that many Christians conceive of – that is, a place where people's souls go when they die – is never mentioned in the Old Testament, and neither is hell.

While there is a word in the Old Testament that describes a place where bodies go when they die, it is not hell. The word I'm referring to is *Sheol*. Sheol is the place of darkness where the dead go. In the Old Testament, it is a place where all the dead go – a grave. Most people are more familiar with the Greek translation of Sheol: Hades. As in, "It's as hot as Hades in here!" In ancient Hebrew traditions, Hades wasn't a place you went to when you died so much as it was a place of nonexistence.

There's a word in the New Testament used by Jesus – *Gehenna* – that meant "a grave." Gehenna also had a geographical location as a valley in Jerusalem. Gehenna was not just a place that meant grave; in ancient times it was believed to have once

80

been a place where child sacrifices were made. And because of that, it had a very bad connotation for the people living in that time. It was considered that anyone buried there had not received a proper burial. For ancient Jews, a proper burial was very important. As the Gospels gained traction in the second part of the first century, those interpreting the word Gehenna defined it as being the place that is opposite of eternal life – that is, a place where the dead are not properly buried, and a place where both the body and the soul go to be destroyed.

In the synoptic Gospels, especially in Mark's Gospel, when Jesus spoke of the Kingdom of God, he was referring to a new kingdom, a paradise, that God was going to put in place on earth. There was going to be a cosmic judgment in the very near future where God was going to destroy those who were evil, and reward those who were righteous with eternal life – on earth. Jesus preached that he was the Son of man who was chosen to rule over this new kingdom as the Messiah when that judgment came. And his disciples would each rule one of the twelve tribes of Israel. All of this was going to take place in a new kingdom – on earth.

One last thing about Jesus' teachings: He never taught that a person's soul would live on after they died. That would have gone against Jewish understanding of the soul. Remember, Jesus was a Jew and he taught from the ancient Jewish books. Jews did in fact believe in a soul; everyone had a soul. However, for the Jews, the soul and the body were literally connected: Neither could live without the other. This understanding comes from the second chapter of Genesis where God breathed life into Adam. For a Jewish person, the soul was like the breath; the soul was what gave the body life. And when the body stopped, when breathing stopped, so did the soul. There was no concept in Jewish teachings that the soul continued after death; in fact, that would have been impossible because once a person died, their soul ceases to be. So there was no

81

place of reward for the soul if the person was good, nor was there a place of punishment for the soul if the person was bad.

Am I making sense so far?

Defense:

Yes, *Doubt*, I think you explained that in a clear way that the jury can understand. Go on.

Doubt:

Ok. I'm going away from the Bible for just a minute, but it will all makes sense, honest.

Ancient Greek philosophers were the first to say there is a body and a distinctive soul. In particular, Plato believed that when the body died, the soul lived on. Some believe this is where the concept of reincarnation began. Again, this wasn't the ancient Hebrew view; this was the view of Greek pagans. When I say, pagans, I'm not referring to an outlaw motorcycle gang! This is a term given to people who did not believe in the one Jewish God. In the time of Jesus, pagans believed in multiple gods; they were polytheists.

There was an ancient Jewish idea that developed a couple of hundred years before Jesus that at the end of time, there was going to be a mass resurrection. At the end of time, in a cosmic judgment when God destroys the forces of evil, he will bring back to life those who were righteous, and those who were righteous will rise (literally, rise from the dead) and have everlasting life on earth. This will be a physical bodily resurrection of the dead who were righteous when they were alive, and they will have eternal life on earth.

The way I like to describe how this idea worked its way into the New Testament is this: Jesus took this ancient Jewish belief and ran with it. Jesus never said evil people would go to hell when this cosmic judgment happened. Instead, Jesus taught that when this judgment occurred, those horrible people would be shown their evil ways, and then they'd be destroyed forever. In contrast, the people who are good would be judged accordingly and their reward would be eternal life – on earth. In short, if you disobeyed God, there would indeed be a punishment, and that punishment was death. Death is permanent, it's eternal. So the punishment was eternal as well.

Are you still with me?

Defense:

We sure are.

Doubt:

I have to talk about a person I've only mentioned in passing up until now, the apostle Paul. Paul is known for a couple of things. He is arguably the most important convert to Christianity, and his letters made their way into the canon of scripture – the New Testament. Paul believed he received both information and instruction from God himself and he went on a mission to establish churches throughout the Roman empire. Paul also believed his talents would best be served if he focused on preaching the good news of Jesus to the gentiles, the pagans. He felt the other apostles could focus on converting Jews to Christianity; he would focus on the gentiles. He even got into arguments with some of the other apostles saying gentiles were just as worthy of salvation through Jesus as the Jews were. This mission took Paul to many Greek communities in his travels.

Paul never met Jesus. Instead of following his teachings, he was busy persecuting the earliest of Christians in the years immediately following the Crucifixion. But when Paul converted to Christianity, he became one of its biggest advocates. Paul believed he would live long enough to meet Jesus in person. This is because of what Jesus said in his teachings. Jesus taught that the Kingdom of God was near and judgment was coming soon. Jesus taught that after his death, he would return to earth.

Paul certainly believed in the Resurrection of Jesus. When Jesus was crucified and his body was no longer in the tomb, he appeared to his disciples. Paul saw the Resurrection of Jesus to mean that the end times were very near and Jesus would definitely be coming back in his lifetime. Jesus is quoted in the Gospels as saying he would return before that generation passed. That is, his second coming would occur before those who heard him preach died. Paul was certain that would happen in his lifetime. Not only was Paul certain of that, he was telling it to everyone during his ministry.

However, as his ministry went on over the decades, it was becoming evident that Jesus was not going to return before that generation died. In fact, many people who believed they would see Jesus at the Second Coming, based in part on what Paul taught, had already died. In Paul's later letters, he developed a new set of beliefs: He would come into the presence of Christ when he died, just as he was in Christ's presence while he was alive. He then taught this to the people he was converting. Since Christ was present in their lives while they were alive, they would be in his presence when they die.

This became the starting point for the idea that even though there wasn't going to be a physical bodily resurrection, and the body will remain dead, the person's soul would go to be with Jesus, who was the Christ. This is the beginning of the concept of Heaven. And if this eternal life of the soul is the reward for those who believed in Jesus, there had to be a punishment for those who didn't. If the soul didn't go to Heaven, there had to be some kind of punishment for the wicked; their soul had to go somewhere – and so, Hades became hell. This is where the concept of hell developed.

Scholars believe the biggest reason why this idea of the soul going to either Heaven or hell caught on is that Paul was teaching and converting Greeks who held the Greek idea (from Plato) that when a person dies, their soul lives on. So the idea of your soul living on with Jesus made sense. They did not see this as a radical idea. Whereas Jewish people believed that the soul ended when the body died, and they would have seen it as a radical belief.

It can be said that if not for Paul, there would not have been the start of the Christian belief in Heaven and hell. Paul basically combined the teachings of Plato, the soul living on after the body dies, with the teachings of Jesus – there will be a judgment at the end of time where there is a resurrection of the dead. I should also state that there are Christians to this day who believe that in addition to the soul going to Heaven or hell, there will be still be a physical resurrection when Jesus returns and judges everyone.

To summarize, it wasn't an ancient Hebrew belief or an Old Testament view that became the Christian view of Heaven and hell. It was the Greek view, a pagan idea, that became the basis for the development of Heaven and hell for Christians. Talk about your paradoxes!

Defense:

I had no idea! Even without this knowledge of the development of Heaven and hell, it's easy to see how you show up when this topic is discussed, or even just thought about.

Doubt:

Yeah, I do tend to hang around this concept a lot. And I must admit that there are times I wish it weren't so. There are times I wish I wasn't there during periods of grief. If ever there are times I've felt unwanted, it's during these times in people's lives. I just hope they understand that just because I'm present, that doesn't have to mean Heaven isn't real. There are plenty of stories from people throughout the ages who have been brought back to life, where they've had a glimpse of the afterlife, and the afterlife seems magnificent. Remember, my purpose isn't to change beliefs, it's to nudge people to dig deeper, to ask questions. And, I think, even during periods of grief, asking questions is a good thing.

Defense:

Doubt, thank you for sharing your sense of vulnerability during times of grief in your testimony.

Doubt:

Just trying to keep it real.

Defense:

All right, why don't we move on to some of the improbabilities and other problems that bring you into people's lives regarding beliefs in the Bible.

The Court:

Counselor, what do you say we take our afternoon break now? I'm sure the jury could use a good stretch and they'd probably like some time to think about everything *Doubt* just testified to; I know I need some time to take it all in.

Defense:

That sounds like a good idea, Your Honor. It will give me some time with my client to streamline the upcoming testimony.

The Court:

Great. We'll take a recess and reconvene once everyone is well rested.

Chapter 6:

Midafternoon Testimony

*Improbabilities * Parables as Lessons * Risks of Reading the Bible Literally * The Jesus Seminar * Confirmation Bias and the Backfire Effect * Problematic Passages * John's Gospel's Anti-Semitic Verse * The Different Endings in Mark's Gospel * The First Two Chapters Added in Luke's Gospel * Jesus Sweats Blood and Is Visited by an Angel in Luke's Gospel*

The Court:

Ladies and gentlemen of the jury, welcome back.

Counselor, are you and your client ready to continue?

Defense:

We are, Your Honor.

The Court:

Okay, then. You may continue with your questioning of *Doubt*.

Defense:

Thank you, Judge.

Doubt, before we took our break, we said we'd start to talk about improbabilities and other problems with the Bible. I want to make sure the jury understands what you mean when you say "other problems." Can you first tell the members of the jury what you mean by problems?

Doubt:

Sure. Maybe it came out wrong when I said problems with the Bible. When I say other problems, I'm not saying I have a problem with the Bible or that the Bible is a problem. That's certainly not the case!

I was just trying to say there are reasons other than contradictions that I show up in the Bible. Some of those reasons are improbabilities and other reasons I show up are — well, they're— See, I can't figure out a word for other reasons I show up, I'm sorry. I can only say that there are some passages that people might find problematic. There, how about instead of saying "other problems," we say there are passages that some people find problematic?

Defense:

That sounds fair. So now that we understand you don't have a problem with the Bible and you don't believe the Bible is a problem, let's talk about some of the improbabilities.

Doubt:

We're going to focus on the New Testament, but I think it's important to at least look at some of the stories in the Old Testament. Just look at the creation story in the Book of Genesis; either story will work. I'm not saying that it's impossible but think of the job Adam had in populating the world! And if we're all descendants of Adam and Eve, how is it possible that this happened without incest? If it was just Adam and Eve, and they had kids, the only way for the next generation to come about would be for their kids to get together. Ew, gross!

And, yes, I've heard the arguments from apologists who have explanations that get around this little detail. But if we're going strictly by what's written, it's not hard to see how some people find this story problematic, as well as improbable.

Then there's the story of Noah and the ark. We're told that he was more than five hundred years old when he started to build it. Most people who remember the story of Noah probably don't recall his age as we have it in the Old Testament. But it's there: five hundred years old.

Even if an ark was built that was to temporarily house every kind of animal, think about the logistics of food and fresh water for the animals, as well as what happens to that food and water after it's been digested. Then, there are the animals themselves. To collect a male and female pair of every known animal is a task that would take more time than building the ark. Animals that were native to that area could be gathered, but what about animals from other parts of the world? How would those animals be corralled and brought to the ark?

And most people don't know that there are contradictions of the flood in the Book of Genesis. In one verse, it says the flood lasted forty days, but a few verses later, it says the flood lasted one hundred fifty days. In one chapter, it says Noah was told to bring two of every kind of animal on board the ark, and in the next chapter, it says Noah was told to take seven pairs of every clean animal and a pair of all the other animals that are not clean.

I know, I know – we're done with contradictions. I just wanted to point out not just an improbability, but that the contradictions make it even more implausible. Most scholars, historians, and anthropologists believe that the story of the great flood, with a five-hundred-year-old man building a boat that held two of every kind of animal, is just that: a story. But it's a story that has lessons in it, and it's the *lessons* in these stories that theologians discuss and debate, then share with those who want to learn from them.

The same can be said about the story of Jonah and the whale. It's from the Book of Jonah in the Old Testament. We're told that as a sign of anger toward Jonah for running away from God, God whipped up a storm while Jonah was at sea. His ship was in peril, and because he knew God did it out of anger, Jonah told the others on the ship to throw him into the ocean. By doing so, Jonah believed the great storm would be calmed. His shipmates obliged his suggestion and threw him overboard. As soon as they did that, the seas became calm. Then God summoned up a large fish that swallowed Jonah whole. Jonah stayed in the fish's belly for three days, reciting a long prayer that was nine verses long. After the third day, God spoke to the fish, and the fish spit out Jonah on to dry land.

The first thing to notice is that nowhere does it say that the fish was a whale. That idea came much later in various translations of the Old Testament. So to say it's the story of Jonah and the whale is a misnomer. But what's relevant here, for the purpose of why we're here, is the improbability of a man surviving being eaten by a fish, let alone living in its belly for three days. If we just use logic and the knowledge we have of sea life and how fish use their gills to extract oxygen from the water in order to live, it doesn't take much to see that a person couldn't survive for that period of time without fresh air.

Once again, most scholars believe this is a story that was told to get people of that time to consider different things about their lives and about the nature of God.

One more example, and then I'll move on to the New Testament.

The Court:

Doubt, we all agreed that you were going to stick to the New Testament.

Doubt:

I know, Your Honor. I am going to the New Testament, I promise. But in order to bring what I want to share into context, it's important to set a foundation of sorts. It will make a lot more sense if I can just use one more example before moving on to the New Testament.

The Court:

One more example, *Doubt*. Just. One. More. Example.

Do you understand?

Doubt:

Yes, Your Honor. And thank you for your understanding and latitude.

The last example I want to share, regarding a story that is improbable, is a construction effort of sorts. It's another story in the Book of Genesis, and it's referred to as the Tower of Babel. The story says that after the great flood, everyone spoke just one language. People decided to build a great city that included a huge tower that would reach to the heavens. By doing this, they would be making a name for themselves.

God comes down to see what they are doing, and after seeing the tower, God confuses their language so they don't understand one another's speech. God then scattered them *across the face of the earth*, as it was written in that chapter of Genesis.

Here is another example, according to the experts, of a story meant to teach a lesson or give understanding regarding something in the lives of the people living at that time. Even with the most modern building techniques of the twenty-first century, I think everyone would agree that it is all but impossible to build a structure tall enough to reach that high in the sky. Scholars have also found similar stories in other cultures from before that time.

Here's why I wanted to share these stories. All of us here today weren't alive when the books of the Bible were written, so we don't have a connection to the traditions and beliefs of that time. Remember, communication was mainly oral; stories were shared among the different villages and went from generation to generation. One of the ways to communicate a lesson that contained a truth in it was to create a story around the truth in order to make the lesson come alive. This was common among the Jewish people: Stories were told in order to share a lesson or to hand down bits of history.

Jesus, as we mentioned earlier, was a Jewish man who lived by the Jewish law after learning it through the customary means of that time. During his life, in the time leading up to his ministry, he was obviously influenced by the dynamics of the oral tradition. In fact, Jesus taught and preached in parables. The Gospels tell us that at least once Jesus said he would only speak in parables to the people in the villages he went to, but he would speak plainly and explain the meaning of the parables with his disciples. Think of how many times Jesus began a story, a parable, with: "There was once a man who…"

A great example of this is the parable of the Good Samaritan. Even if you're not familiar with the particulars of the story, everyone has at least heard of the good Samaritan. Anyone reading that part of Luke's Gospel can see right away that Jesus wasn't telling a factual historical event; he was offering a story with a lesson in it that he hoped his listeners would think about.

I hope this all makes sense so far.

Defense:

Yes, *Doubt*, it does make sense. And maybe you can tell the members of the jury why you wanted to share that with them.

Doubt:

I wanted to share these stories and explain why they were told and written as parts of the Old Testament. Even though we're talking about contradictions and passages that are problematic, it is important to understand that these stories had a sacred importance in the lives of the people of that day as well as readers of them in our present time. We shouldn't discount the importance of these stories and

> *Reading the Bible literally as the inerrant and infallible word of God often leads to hardened hearts and closed minds. We sometimes need to look past the words and see the message contained in the story.*

passages just because we find them improbable, because they all contain lessons to consider or they point toward an understanding of God. We sometimes need to look past the words and see the message contained in the story. Literalism is something scholars wrangle with when they're explaining the historical aspects of the books of the Bible.

I want the members of the jury, each member, to understand that as we move forward talking about what I call problems in the Bible, every passage we discuss was written with a purpose. It was important for the writers of those times to tell what they told. No matter how problematic or improbable we see them now, these passages were very important and had significance for a lesson or an understanding of God.

Regardless of their historical accuracy, please consider the lessons in them or the understanding they were trying to convey. It's much easier to simply read a Bible passage and accept it all as factual and historically accurate, and then to look deeper into it and think about the message the writer was trying to convey. Reading the Bible literally as the inerrant and infallible word of God often leads to hardened hearts and closed minds.

Defense:

So are you saying we shouldn't take any of the passages in the Bible literally? Are you saying none of what's written on the pages of the Bible actually happened?

Doubt:

No, not at all! I'm saying we need to take into account the traditions and customs of a culture that none of us has experienced and consider what was acceptable back then. We also need to accept the fact, again, that we have no original manuscripts of any of the books of the Bible, and what we do have as Gospels are copies of copies that were written decades after Jesus was crucified.

Defense:

So how can anyone know if the events that are written about, or even what Jesus said, really happened? Are the members of the jury to assume that we're just supposed to flip a coin and let chance decide what's true and what isn't?

Doubt:

Let me answer that this way:

A growing number of people – laypeople, clergy, and professors who teach at seminaries around the world – say the stories in the Bible aren't so much about historical authenticity as they are about the messages and lessons contained in them. In fact, people in the Church and in the institutions that train those headed for ministry have been saying this for decades. Their biggest concern is that if the Church doesn't stop insisting on taking everything in the Bible literally, Christianity is in danger of becoming an irrelevant religion. These people are saying, and have been saying, that if the Church keeps insisting that the unbelievable stories in the Bible are factually true, membership in the Church will decline at such a rate that it won't ever be able to recover.

> *If the Church doesn't stop insisting on taking everything in the Bible literally, Christianity is in danger of becoming an irrelevant religion.*

I've known these people who are advocating a nonliteral reading of the Bible for a long time. Some of them invited me into their lives, while others did all they could to kick me out of their homes — and churches. Some of these people have cursed me when I first came into their lives, while others welcomed me and were glad I was a part of their faith journey. Yet here's the thing that people have a hard time believing: My presence in the lives of the people I'm talking about didn't end up diluting their faith or, worse yet, taking it away altogether. Instead, they developed a deeper understanding of the meaning behind the stories and this, for the most part, deepened their faith in many ways.

Defense:

Okay. But that doesn't answer my question. How can anyone know if the stories in the Bible, and the words of Jesus, are accurate?

Doubt:

My best answer probably isn't the best answer for the jury. At least the answer that makes it easy for them. The truth is it's not for me to answer that question; each person must come to their own answer, at their own time. Whether through research, reading books, attending different places of worship

– whatever method is used – each one of us is ultimately responsible for our own thoughts, opinions, and beliefs. My purpose in life isn't to give anyone simple answers. It's meant to be those ants in the pants of those who are paying attention.

That being said, I might be able to offer something for the members of the jury to think about. I know when we were talking during the break you said it would be brought up later, but now seems like a better time to talk about it.

Defense:

We talked about a couple of things in order to keep this trial moving along. To what are you referring, *Doubt?*

Doubt:

I'm talking about the Jesus Seminar.

Defense:

Well, since you brought it up, you might as well explain to the members of the jury what the Jesus Seminar is and its bearing on this trial.

Doubt:

The Jesus Seminar was active from about 1985 until the beginning of this century. It was a group of about 150 people researching the teachings and deeds of Jesus as they are described in the Gospels. These were scholars, clergy members, and people from all walks of life and from various Christian denominations who gathered for more than fifteen years to

> *Members of the Jesus Seminar researched and debated each and every action and saying of Jesus, then voted on whether they were historical and factual.*

determine which deeds and words of Jesus were historically accurate. They researched and debated each and every action

96

and saying of Jesus, then voted on whether they were historical and factual.

Of course, it's impossible to determine with absolute certainty if Jesus said or didn't say something. There were no tape recorders or video cameras back in his day, and there weren't any cable news channels to cover his ministry. As I've said repeatedly, all scholars have to rely on are copies of the ancient manuscripts that became known as the Gospels. So the members of the Jesus Seminar voted on each saying or deed in one of four ways:

1. Jesus did or said something that was very likely true.
2. Jesus did or said something that might have been true.
3. Jesus did or said something that probably wasn't true.
4. Jesus did or said something that was very unlikely to be true.

After meeting for fifteen years, all the votes were in: The group concurred that about 18 percent of what's written in the Gospels was actually said or done by Jesus. That's only 18 percent – as in a little less than 20 percent. So the members concluded that less than one-in-five sayings or deeds of Jesus, as recorded in the Gospels, is likely to be historically accurate.

It is important for the members of the jury to know that there are scholars and theologians who vehemently disagree with the findings of the Jesus Seminar. While most of them don't argue that every word in the Bible – every saying and every account – really happened, they do argue that 18 percent is too low a number. Other scholars agree with the number but disagree which 18 percent is the correct 18 percent. In other words, while they agree that about one-in-five is the right percentage, they believe different deeds and sayings are the historically correct ones. And so, the debate continues.

My reason for mentioning the findings of the Jesus Seminar is not to offer it as absolute proof that less than one-in-five words of Jesus in the Gospels were really said by him; instead, it's another piece of the puzzle for people to consider when I show up in their lives. They can look at the puzzle piece and work on figuring out where it goes, or they can discard it as having no value. Again, it doesn't concern me one way or the other what anyone does with the information I shed light on. It's up to each person to determine what to do with information as it becomes known to them.

Defense:

So just to be clear, you're not saying that eighteen is a proven percentage of what is historically accurate as to the sayings and deeds of Jesus. You're offering that percentage as a finding of research conducted by experts in their fields. Is that correct?

Doubt:

Exactly. I'll say it again: There is no way to determine, as being 100 percent certain, as to what Jesus said or did in his lifetime. What biblical scholars, historians, and anthropologists do is look at what's written in the New Testament and compare it to the manuscripts that have survived to this point in time. They compare those manuscripts to other known writings that didn't make it into the New Testament, as well as what they know about the culture and traditions of that time in ancient Middle Eastern history. Then, using their combined knowledge and experience, they decide what is more probable or likely to have been said or done by Jesus.

Defense:

Is there a way this information can be used in a way other than as a definitive "he did something or didn't do something" platform?

Doubt:

> You mean instead of relying on the findings of the Jesus Seminar as the Gospel truth?
>
> Sorry, I've been waiting to use that one all day!

Defense:

> Yes, instead of suggesting it is the Gospel truth, can the members of the jury use this information in a way that can help them, other than having to decide if it is true or not?

Doubt:

> There *is* another way the jury can use this information. If they use it as a foundation for the rest of this trial, I think it will help them when considering passages from the New Testament. In fact, this information can help them, if they choose, even after this trial is over.

Defense:

> What do you mean as a foundation for considering passages from the New Testament for the rest of this trial?

Doubt:

> Obviously, we're going to be covering more material and some of it might cause angst in some of the jury. If the members would allow themselves to consider at least the possibility that only a small percentage of what was written down was actually said or done by Jesus, they should be able to look at my testimony through a different lens – from a different perspective. Instead of having to choose between believing what they've learned since Sunday school or believing my testimony, they can at least accept that a group of experts determined that not everything that was written in the Bible really happened. Accepting that premise can serve as a foundation and it will allow them to set aside any preconceived

thoughts as well as temper being shocked by learning something that goes against their beliefs. And that – learning and accepting something that goes against our beliefs – is something that really is hard to do.

Defense:

Hard in what way?

Doubt:

Okay, let me explain.

We've all heard of *confirmation bias*, right? It's the phenomenon when we only seek out information that confirms our own biases. It's where we only watch certain sides of the news – we only tune into cable news outlets on one side of the political spectrum and refuse to watch the other side's news outlets. We feed what we already like, and we aren't interested in finding out what's on the other side of the coin, so to speak.

Confirmation bias can be dangerous if used in areas of our life where an open and unbiased mind is needed. Think about medical research. If the researchers were only looking for results that support their claim that their latest device really does work, they would be dismissing all the other data that showed it wasn't working the way they hoped or showed it produced harmful side effects. We want – we demand – that the medical profession be completely unbiased when it comes to research. Their confirmation bias could potentially be deadly.

In the same way some medical researchers might try to protect their newest developments, we humans have a sort of built-in device that protects us; it's called our unconscious, or subconscious, mind. Our subconscious mind does everything it can to protect us from feeling or doing things that go against our beliefs. And it's on an unconscious level that confirmation bias takes place. So in order to protect us from information that might go against our beliefs, our subconscious mind forms all those thoughts that make us believe those other news outlets are trash. By doing so, we don't have any desire to tune in, and in fact, we have a very strong desire to bash them whenever we're talking with our peers.

Researchers found that when information is presented that goes against strongly held beliefs, the part of the brain responsible for self-preservation becomes active.

There's another trick our subconscious mind has up its sleeve if information that goes against our beliefs somehow gets past all the barriers and makes its way to our eyes and ears. Social scientists call this the *backfire effect*. Using functional MRIs, researchers have been able to watch – in real time – what parts of the brain become active when information is presented that goes against strongly held beliefs. When new information is presented to a person, one would expect the parts of the brain that are responsible for learning would become active. What the researchers found, however, is when that information is the opposite of a strongly held belief, the part of the brain responsible for self-preservation becomes active instead. When this type of information was presented to the people who volunteered for the study, the part of the primal brain that's responsible for our fight-or-flight response became very active.

And this is interesting: When the volunteers were shown that the new information was 100 percent correct and their previous belief was 100 percent wrong, that primal part of the brain became even more active and the volunteers dug in their heels and insisted with even more vigor that their original belief was the right belief. Even in the face of evidence that absolutely disproved their belief, people became firmer in their stance on the topic. And the two topics that caused the most pushback? Politics and religion.

The study showed that when strongly held political or religious beliefs were shown to be untrue, the part of the brain responsible for self-preservation became the most active. As an example, if someone who believed you have to wait at least a half an hour before you can go swimming was shown facts that refuted that belief, there was only minor activity in that part of the primal brain. But if information was given that showed, unequivocally, that a previously held religious belief was false, the primal brain became very active. This is what researchers have called the backfire effect.

> *Even in the face of evidence that absolutely disproved their strongly held political or religious belief, people became firmer in their stance on the topic.*

This is why I said it is hard to accept new information that goes against previously held beliefs, especially religious beliefs. It doesn't mean there's something wrong with you if you become anxious or frustrated with me. Even if you become angry at me and tell me I'm going to hell for sharing what I'm sharing, know that those feelings are starting at an unconscious level. And it probably means you are normal!

Defense:

So what you're saying is the members of the jury should—

Doubt:

They should be gentle with themselves.

Defense:

That sounds like good advice, *Doubt*.

Doubt:

Every now and then I get good wood on the ball.

Defense:

> Let's continue with what you said are some problematic passages.

Doubt:

> Okay. How about we begin with some passages that leave you scratching your head?

Defense:

> Go right ahead.

Doubt:

> Here is a list of sorts of just some of the laws from the Bible, starting with the Old Testament:
>
> - If a child is willfully disobedient to a parent, she or he shall be stoned to death; I don't know how many of us would be here right now if that law was followed by our parents.
> - You can't have a variety of crops in your garden; so much for planting cucumbers and tomatoes in your backyard.
> - You can't eat shellfish; there goes Red Lobster.
> - You can't wear clothes made of more than one fiber; so much for those comfortable-fitting underpants.
> - Men can't cut their hair or shave their beards; I know a couple of guys who would be okay with this.
> - A man can't share a bed with his wife if she is menstruating; maybe this is why twin beds were invented.
> - You can't eat anything that mixes meat and dairy; there goes a good cheeseburger.
> - If you're blind, or lame, or have a mutilated face, you can't go to the altar and receive Holy Communion; maybe those people sleep late on Sundays and don't mind missing church.

- If a priest has a daughter who is a prostitute, she must be burnt at the stake; that should do the trick for putting the fear of God into adolescent girls.

- Anyone in your family who suggests worshipping a different god shall be put to death; so much for engaging in open family discussions.

- And finally, anyone who has sex with their mother-in-law shall be put to death; I don't even want to think about why this law was put on the books.

This is just a sampling of the list of laws that can be found in the Old Testament. The reason I bring them up is to point out how dangerous it can be to take everything in the Bible literally. If we were to follow the letter of every law in the Bible, we'd probably all be in jail. There are 613 commandments in the Old Testament – 613 laws that say what can and cannot be done, what should and should not be done. And, yes, 613 is lot more than the ten commandments Moses mentioned.

We need to understand that these laws developed over time to separate the Jewish people from others. It was their way of having a unique identity that showed their obedience to God. Sitting here today, you and I can say they are outdated, that they are no longer relevant. And I don't think anyone would argue with us. Here's the thing, though: If these laws are outdated, what else in the Bible is outdated? And who are we to determine what laws we should keep and which ones are no longer important? Aren't we playing God if we set out to make a list of which ones stay and which ones go?

> When we probe beyond the words themselves and look at what the message is, the Bible becomes more than a manual to live by. It becomes a living piece of wonderful stories – stories filled with errors and problems. And I would submit that it's those errors and problems that mirror human life more than our expectations of godly perfection.

These are, of course, rhetorical questions, but they point out the problem with biblical literalism. We either say the entire Bible is without errors and its word is infallible, or we look at what was behind the words that were being written. When we probe beyond the words themselves and take the time to look at what the message is, the Bible becomes more than a manual to live by. It becomes a living piece of wonderful stories – stories filled with errors and problems. And I would submit that it's those errors and problems that mirror human life more than our expectations of godly perfection.

Defense:

Doubt, I'm sure everyone would agree that these laws are antiquated, and no one should try to live by them today. These are the laws in the Old Testament. Before we move on to the New Testament, are there any other passages in the Old Testament that are problematic?

Doubt:

There are. But for the sake of time, I'll only mention one. And it's a doozy! I can't imagine any member of the clergy building a sermon around it.

It's a Psalm. When people think of the Book of Psalms, they usually think of the poetic flow of verses either crying out to God or praising God. Most people, even if they're not religious, have heard of the twenty-third Psalm. It's arguably one of the most-read passages in the Bible: "The Lord is my shepherd...."

However, there are some Psalms in the same book as the twenty-third Psalm that make you wonder how they even got there. One Psalm passage that, on the surface, people would look at as horrific is found in Psalm 137:7-9. Here it is as it's written:

"Remember, O LORD, against the Edomites the day of Jerusalem's fall, how they said, 'Tear it down! Tear it down! Down to its foundations!' O daughter Babylon, you devastator! Happy shall they be who pay you back what you have done to us! Happy shall they be who take your little ones and dash them against the rock!'"

Take a look at that last line: "Happy shall they be who take your little ones and dash them against the rock!" What this passage is saying is that we should find joy in bashing the little children of our enemies against the rocks – killing the children of our enemies. Didn't Jesus teach that we are to love our enemies?

Biblical scholars and theologians look at this text and they remind us that we have to first have an understanding of what was going on at the time it was written. Then we need to read it in its historical context because, as they argue, this isn't about smashing babies against rocks. Instead, it's about retribution against an evil enemy that was not so much a person or persons as it was an empire or kingdom that invaded and destroyed their land.

I agree with the scholars and theologians who say before judging this passage, one must first have a historical background on what was happening, and what had happened, when this Psalm was written. Then the reader needs to read not just the words, but to understand

Most of us have very little, if any, knowledge of ancient Middle Eastern culture and traditions. Yet we pick up a Bible and assume we'll understand everything written in it for no other reason than we comprehend and know how to read words in English.

what the writer was trying to convey when he wrote it – that is, to read it in the context in which it was written, and to not take it literally.

Doesn't that sound like what I said earlier? We – all of us sitting here – have very little, if any, knowledge of culture and traditions of the ancient Middle East. And yet, we pick up a Bible and assume we'll understand everything written in it if for no other reason than we comprehend and know how to read words in the English language. But as we just saw, it's not as simple as that.

I wanted to bring this up now because as we move on to the New Testament, I think it would be wise if we all kept the same open-mindedness we had when we looked at archaic laws in the Old Testament, as well as a troubling passage that made it into the Book of Psalms.

Defense:

I knew there were some weird laws or rules in the Old Testament, but I had no idea that a passage in the Psalms was one of them. And when I say, "weird laws," I'm not suggesting that there was something wrong with them way back then. I'm simply saying that by today's standards, they seem strange. But that passage from Psalm 137 – I'm almost speechless.

The Court:

Counselor, your job basically mandates that you are anything but speechless, and your role here isn't to give commentary to your client's testimony. Move on with the questions and stick to just asking questions.

Defense:

Yes, Your Honor. I apologize.

Doubt, can you share some of, at least what you consider to be, problematic passages in the New Testament?

Doubt:

Sure. Can I recite it as a bulleted list like I did with the Old Testament?

Defense:

Absolutely.

Doubt:

All right. Here are some of the laws spelled out in the New Testament:

- Slaves must be obedient and submissive to their masters; unfortunately, this passage was used to justify slavery in the United States.
- Women must be submissive to their husbands; this, unfortunately, has been used to justify spousal abuse.
- Women must be quiet in church and hold no position of authority in church; this passage has been used to keep women out of the ministry in certain denominations.
- Women cannot have any position of authority over men; this is another passage that's been used to suppress the business success of women.
- Women must wear a hat when they're in church, however, men can't pray when they're wearing a hat; okay, I have no idea why this was needed.

I need to note that none of the laws I just mentioned from the New Testament came from Jesus. These appear in various letters, called epistles, from different people writing to other people or churches during the early development of Christianity. But they do show what can happen if we insist on a literal reading of the Bible.

While those laws weren't given by Jesus, there is one law Jesus gave that is problematic. It's problematic because Jesus himself broke it after he said it, as did Paul who spoke openly about knowing what Jesus taught. In Matthew's Gospel, Jesus tells those listening that they shouldn't be angry with their brother or sister, and if they call someone a fool they will be cast into the fires of death.

The problem is, one chapter after telling people they shouldn't call anyone a fool, Jesus calls the Pharisees and scribes fools. In his letter to the Galatians, Paul told the Galatians they were foolish. So if Jesus taught that others shouldn't be called fools, why did he later call the Pharisees and the scribes fools? And if Paul knew the teachings of Jesus, why did he call the Galatians foolish?

As with other passages in the Bible, there are scholars and theologians who explain this contradiction by once more talking about context and the need to understand what Jesus really meant. And they probably are right. But here we are again with a passage from the Bible where we are asked to consider the context in light of a certain historical period while grasping at what Jesus actually meant. If that's the case, shouldn't theologians recommend that readers of the New Testament use the same reasoning – apply known history for context?

I'm not trying to create arguments or controversy with these questions. That's not my purpose in people's lives. If I can give someone who's reading the Bible a reason to think about what's in the pages between the covers in a way other than literalism, I think I've done my job. If the members of the jury recall the percentage given by the Jesus Seminar, maybe this passage won't be as hard to grasp as it is interesting to ponder.

Defense:

That's good advice, *Doubt*. Are there any other places in the New Testament that people have a problem with?

Doubt:

There are plenty! Most atheists will tell you they have a problem with just about all the New Testament. But if you're asking me to offer another example where the everyday reader of the Bible might have a problem, I do think there's one more to consider.

Defense:

And it's from the New Testament?

Doubt:

Yes, from John's Gospel.

To fully understand it, I need to share some background. I'd like to share some historical reference so the jury can understand the context in which it was written. Your Honor, I swear I'll stay on point and be brief!

If you recall from my testimony this morning, I described how each Gospel was written with its own theme. The main theme of John's Gospel is to prove the divinity of Jesus. Unlike the synoptic Gospels, John's Gospel has long monologues given by Jesus where he comes right out and says he is the Son of God. In these passages, and in other chapters and verses in John's Gospel, Jesus is clearly comparing himself with God.

For example, John's Gospel is the only Gospel where Jesus uses the *I am* term, where Jesus begins sentences with, "I am…." [See John 6:35; and other chapters and verses]

This is a reference to the Old Testament's story of Moses asking God what he should call God. Moses asks God, "What's your name?" God replies: "I AM WHO I AM." [Exodus 3:14] God then tells Moses to tell the people *I am* has sent you.

Scholars and theologians have often discussed the reason or reasons why the writers of John's Gospel focused on the divinity of Jesus. One possibility was because of the decades that had passed from the fall of Jerusalem until the Gospel was written. Remember, John's Gospel was the last Gospel written. And that passing of time allowed for stories and opinions to be passed down from earlier generations – stories about Jesus and the fall of Jerusalem and the destruction of the Temple. Jerusalem fell to the Roman army in the year 70 of the Common Era. That left about twenty-five years before John's Gospel was written (around 95 C.E.).

It's important to remember that Jews were the first people who learned about Jesus' teachings, so they were the first to accept his messages and adopt his beliefs. During the period before John's Gospel was written, some Jews accepted Jesus' messages and adopted his beliefs, while others refuted them and stuck to traditional teachings and readings in their synagogues. When Jerusalem was overrun – when it fell to the Romans and their Temple was destroyed – some of the Jews who accepted Jesus' message and who were by then his followers blamed the fall of Jerusalem on the Jews who did not accept Jesus and who denied that he was the Messiah. His followers blamed the nonbelievers for this because, in their view, they had not only denied the Messiah that God had sent them, but they killed him, too. And so, God had punished them all by allowing the Roman army to defeat them and for the Temple to be destroyed.

So there was a rift in the communities and in the synagogues over who was to blame for the fall of Jerusalem. The Jews who had decided to follow Jesus blamed the Jews who rejected him for their defeat and also for the now two-plus decades of chaos they were living in. As this divide grew deeper, so too did the rhetoric as the traditional Jews were being called "God killers." God had sent them a new Messiah – Jesus – and they killed him.

111

With all that as a background, there is now some historical context for the passage I want to share with the members of the jury. See, Your Honor, I told you I could stay on point and keep it brief.

The Court:

Great. Let's see how long we can keep this streak going.

Defense:

Umm, *Doubt*, why don't you explain to the jury the passage you want to discuss?

Doubt:

Staying on point, sure.

The passage is from the eighth chapter of John's Gospel [John 8:42-45] and, like I said earlier, it's one that's been used to fuel antisemitism and hate crimes for a long, long time. The passage is this:

> Jesus said to them, "If God were your Father, you would love me, for I came from God and now I am here. I did not come on my own, but he sent me. Why do you not understand what I say? It is because you cannot accept my word. You are from your father the devil, and you choose to do your father's desires. He was a murderer from the beginning and does not stand in the truth, because there is no truth in him. When he lies, he speaks according to his own nature, for he is a liar and the father of lies. But because I tell the truth, you do not believe me."

In this passage, Jesus is talking to "the Jews" about their father being God. There's an exchange between Jesus and the Jews he was speaking to, and the Jews said they are descendants of Abraham, so Abraham is their father. [John 8:39] And that's when Jesus lays this on them. Some people miss it; it appears subtle if you're not looking for it. In case you missed it, Jesus is calling the Jews "children of the devil." He says their father is the devil. He then accuses them of choosing their father's desires – of choosing the desires of the devil. And because the devil is a liar, they don't believe Jesus.

More than a few people find this passage to be the most troubling of all the passages in the New Testament. How can Jesus, a Jew himself, speak so harshly of his own people? How can he call them children of the devil? If one were to read this literally, they might be inclined to deal with Jewish people the way they would deal with someone whose father is the devil. And, unfortunately, they have.

Hitler's *Mein Kampf* includes these quotes:

> "Hence today I believe that I am acting in accordance with the will of the Almighty Creator; by defending myself against the Jew, I am fighting for the work of the Lord."

> "And the founder of Christianity made no secret indeed of his estimation of the Jewish people. When He found it necessary, He drove those enemies of the human race out of the Temple of God."

> "His [the Jewish person's] life is only of this world, and his spirit is inwardly as alien to true Christianity as his nature two thousand years previous was to the great founder of the new doctrine. Of course, the latter made no secret of his attitude toward the Jewish people, and when necessary he even took the whip to drive from the temple of the Lord this adversary of all humanity…"

While he never cites John's Gospel, or any other book of the Bible, in this and other writings, it's not hard to see that Hitler's

113

hatred of the Jewish people has firm roots in his interpretation of Christianity. Unfortunately, that hatred didn't stop with the end of the war. From that time up to our present day, anti-Semitic hate groups have claimed Christianity as their religion and as the basis for their actions. I must reiterate what I shared earlier: Biblical literalism can be, and often is, dangerous.

Defense:

Just to be clear for the members of the jury: You're not saying that John's Gospel is responsible for Hitler's actions, correct?

Doubt:

That is absolutely correct! I'm not saying, nor even suggesting, that John's Gospel is to blame for the hatred in Hitler's heart. It is much broader than that. Hitler wasn't the first and he wasn't the last to cherry-pick passages from the New Testament and use them to further

> *There is a real danger in choosing only those passages that confirm our own biases to create in our minds the nature of Jesus.*

their cause. What I am saying is that there is a real danger in choosing only those passages that confirm our own biases to create in our minds the nature of Jesus.

If we understood the messages and lessons behind and within the words written in the New Testament, we would come away with a picture of Jesus and his teachings that transcend the rhetoric of those who claim to know what God says. I was just using Hitler as an example because I don't think there's anyone alive who hasn't heard of him and his hatred toward Jewish people.

Defense:

Thank you for sharing that with the jury. I wanted to make sure they understood what you were saying.

Let's move away from hatred and discuss other passages that are problematic. What are some other passages that have issues that might be interesting for the jury to hear?

Doubt:

Some passages that appear in the books of the New Testament weren't found in the earliest manuscripts. You might recall that earlier I talked about the passage about the woman caught in adultery in John's Gospel and the Johannine Comma found in the letter called First John. These passages were almost certainly added by scribes to earlier manuscripts while they were being copied. Well, there are other examples of additions to manuscripts that are interesting.

I'll start with the first Gospel that was written, Mark's Gospel. Remember, Mark's Gospel is one of the synoptic Gospels that, along with Matthew's and Luke's Gospels, recount the ministry and death of Jesus. When these Gospels are read, stories from one Gospel's account seem familiar with the same account told in another of the synoptic Gospels. When things seem familiar, we tend to miss subtle nuances such as footnotes or other punctuation notations that suggest we dig deeper.

Since all three synoptic Gospels detail Jesus' death and resurrection, we assume that's the way they were written during the second half of the first century. However, the truth is, that's not what happened. Biblical scholars are almost united in believing that Mark's Gospel originally ended at the eighth verse in chapter 16. However, there are actually twenty verses in that chapter. How can that be?

The answer is that the last twelve verses in Mark's Gospel [Mark 16: 9-20] were added by a scribe or scribes. This isn't my answer; this is the answer given by experts who've devoted their careers to studying the Bible and the ancient manuscripts that are the basis for its existence. These experts say Mark's

Gospel originally ended where the women flee the tomb in fear. Verse 8 reads like this:

> "So they went out and fled from the tomb, for terror and amazement had seized them; and they said nothing to anyone, for they were afraid."

One only needs to look at the ends of the other two synoptic Gospels to see there's a problem here. The other two synoptic Gospels tell of Jesus' resurrection and his subsequent interaction with his disciples. Anyone reading Matthew's or Luke's Gospel and then reading Mark's Gospel would certainly wonder what happened at the end. The book ends abruptly with the women running off in fear. There's no closure, not even a hint of what happened to Jesus' body. Without Jesus appearing to his disciples after the Resurrection, anyone reading Mark's Gospel could only speculate – did the women go to the wrong tomb, or maybe it was an instance of grave robbing?

And if this were the only Gospel we had, if the other three Gospels were never written, Christianity would probably have been just another fringe Jewish offshoot that would go nowhere. Just imagine if Mark's Gospel was the only Gospel written, and it ended with the women running off in fear – rather than describing the Resurrection.

> *Imagine if Mark's Gospel was the only Gospel and had ended without describing the Resurrection.*

This seems to have been an issue with some scribes who were copying Mark's manuscript after the Gospels of Matthew and Luke started making the rounds through area synagogues. It also needs to be noted that the apostle Paul, who was writing ten to twenty years *before* Mark's Gospel was written, was teaching others about Jesus' resurrection and his appearance to his disciples. What's a scribe to do when he's asked to copy a manuscript that is not in line with two other Gospels that are circulating – a manuscript that is incomplete with what is being told about the death of Jesus?

The answer appears to be that the scribe should add an ending that agrees with the oral tradition of the time and coincides with the other two Gospels. So the final twelve verses in Mark that appear in later manuscripts are coming *after* the earliest verses known to scholars. These verses describe Jesus' appearance to his disciples, what they did with that experience, and his ascension to Heaven.

But the problem with this passage doesn't quite end there.

Defense:

What do you mean it doesn't quite end there?

Doubt:

There is at least one manuscript that has a different ending than the one contained in the additional last twelve verses of Mark's Gospel. Because of that, most Bibles include two alternate endings of Mark's Gospel called "The Shorter Ending of Mark" and "The Longer Ending of Mark."

The shorter ending of Mark's Gospel is:

> "And all that had been commanded them they told briefly to those around Peter. And afterward Jesus himself sent out through them, from east to west, the sacred and imperishable proclamation of eternal salvation."

There is no verse number assigned to it, so it's assumed to be a continuation of the eighth verse.

None of the wording in the shorter ending appears anywhere in the longer ending. Again, the longer ending has twelve verses that detail who Jesus appeared to, what he said to them, what they did, and his ascension. So it's conceivable that there are three different ways Mark's Gospel ends. And each ending leaves the reader with a different idea of Jesus' death and resurrection. In just about every Bible, there is a footnote explaining the last twelve verses in Mark's Gospel as well as containing both the shorter and longer endings.

Defense:

It's hard to believe that many people may not be aware of this. At least, as far as we know, it's the only place where an ending was added to a story. Are there any examples where something was added to the beginning of a New Testament book?

Doubt:

It's almost as if we planned this, isn't it? Yes, there is an example where something was added to the beginning of a Gospel. And it's not just a handful of verses, it's two complete chapters!

Defense:

Two chapters? Added to the beginning of a Gospel? This has got to be good.

Doubt:

It's something that's not that well known – even among some clergy and within the Church. Remember that two of the three synoptic Gospels tell the story of Jesus' birth, referred to as the birth narratives. Both narratives begin with the genealogy of Jesus' father, Joseph, then give the birth story. However, biblical scholars are aware of manuscripts that predate the manuscripts that were used to write what we now call the Gospel of Luke. These earlier manuscripts were not widely circulated, and the area where they were circulated was in a different part of the empire than the more widely disseminated manuscripts that were used for Luke's Gospel as we have it today.

118

That alone might not be enough for someone to think that what we have today isn't the way the Gospel was meant to be from the beginning. It's not until you look at how the third chapter in Luke's Gospel begins that questions arise. In the manuscripts that predate the ones used for Luke's Gospel as it appears in our Bibles today, the third chapter in Luke's Gospel was actually the first chapter.

When you look at the first verse of the third chapter, it appears to be the start of a book, not the beginning of a chapter. It reads like this: "In the fifteenth year of the reign of Emperor Tiberius, when Pontius Pilate was governor of Judea...." It then goes on to talk about John the Baptist and the prophecy of Isaiah that there will be a voice crying out in the wilderness. It then continues to the baptism of Jesus and to the start of his ministry.

This is almost identical to how Mark's Gospel begins. Marks' Gospel, the first Gospel written, does not have an account of the birth of Jesus. It begins with John the Baptist sharing the prophecy of Isaiah, then goes to Jesus' baptism and to his ministry. If one were to place the beginning of the first chapter of Mark's Gospel and the beginning of the third chapter of Luke's Gospel side by side, they would see just how similar they are. And if you were to read the last verses of the second chapter of Luke's Gospel and go right into the first verse of the third chapter, you'd see that unlike the other chapters in Luke's Gospel, there isn't a smooth transition between the end of chapter 2 and the beginning of chapter 3.

Defense:

So it looks like the scribes once again added something to give their take on how Jesus should be portrayed, right?

Doubt:

Actually, this time scholars say that's not the case. Scholars and writing experts have determined with a reasonable degree of certainty that the person who wrote Luke's Gospel also wrote the first two chapters. There are theories as to why the writer would have omitted anything about Jesus' birth when he first sat down and penned it, only to write the birth story into later manuscripts after some years had passed.

One of those theories is that the writer wanted to show that Jesus was divine since his conception, not his baptism. Another reason might have been to show the *humanness* of Jesus; to show that Jesus was indeed a human and not a ghost, it was important to have a description of his birth. But since we can't interview the writer of Luke's Gospel, all we have are theories and suppositions.

Defense:

Theories or suppositions without a foundation aren't allowed in court testimony, so let's move one.

Is there anything else about this Gospel that's noteworthy for the members of the jury to consider?

Doubt:

Yes, and I just thought of it!

I should have brought it up when I was talking about changes to the manuscripts made by the scribes. I just thought of it when I said one of the theories for the chapters being added was to show the humanness of Jesus. Can I mention it now?

Defense:

Go right ahead.

Doubt:

I was saying just a minute ago that one of the possible reasons the writer of Luke's Gospel went back and added the first two chapters was to show that Jesus was real and not a ghost. That's because there was a sect of Christianity that believed Jesus only appeared to be human; this group believed that since Jesus was God, he couldn't possibly be human as well. This group mainly used Luke's Gospel for that reason. This is why some scholars believe the writer of Luke added the first two chapters after the manuscript was completed. As this group gained some traction, other groups spoke out against it, saying their teaching, and understanding of Jesus being a ghost, was heresy.

I told you all that to tell you this: There is a passage toward the end of Luke's Gospel that has two verses in it that aren't found in the oldest manuscripts of the Gospel. Scholars believe these two verses were added by a scribe to refute the notion that Jesus wasn't human. If a scribe wanted to show that Jesus was indeed human, one of the ways to do that would be to show that Jesus had blood pumping through his body.

The verses I'm talking about show up toward the end of Luke's Gospel, in the twenty-second chapter [Luke 22: 43-44]. The passage is Jesus praying just before his arrest. That passage includes this: "Then an angel from heaven appeared to him and gave him strength. In his anguish he prayed more earnestly, and his sweat became like great drops of blood falling to the ground." Here, Jesus' sweat was like blood.

I should add that another reason the early Christian group believed Jesus couldn't be human was because in Luke's Gospel, he really doesn't suffer the way he does in other Gospel accounts of his crucifixion. Remember, in Luke's account of the Crucifixion, Jesus asks God to forgive those who are nailing him to the cross and is able to have a coherent conversation with a criminal who is hanging on a cross next to him. There isn't the anguish and depiction of pain in Luke's Gospel as in the others.

Unless Jesus had some kind of superhuman strength, this offshoot group argued that Jesus would have surely suffered and had a more emotional response than to calmly go to the cross and then die without the agony described in the other

Gospels. So of course Jesus was calm and suffered very little; God had sent an angel to give him strength to endure what he was about to experience. Scholars believe a possible reason the scribe added the verse saying an angel gave him strength was to refute the argument given by this group that Jesus wasn't human.

Defense:

There really is so much more to the books of the Bible than just reading each line and assuming we understand everything, isn't there?

Doubt, let's now move on to other books in the New Testament.

The Court:

Counselor, we've been going hard since the afternoon break. I think this would be a good place to end the day's testimony and recess for the day. Let's pick it up tomorrow morning after we've all had a good night's rest and we can return refreshed.

Defense:

I was hoping you'd make that executive decision. I know I'm hungry and am looking forward to—

Doubt:

I'm starving!

The Court:

All right, everyone, we'll call it a day and resume *Doubt's* testimony tomorrow morning.

Chapter 7:

Day 2 Testimony Begins

*Moving a Colon to Fit a Prophecy * The Walking Dead in Matthew's Gospel *
Names of the Disciples * Number of Disciples Alive at the Resurrection * Paul's
Omission of Judas * Gospel of Peter's Omission of the Death of Judas * The
Story of Judas Compared to a Mythical Story * Paul's Omission of an Empty
Tomb * The Apostle Paul and His Ministry * Paul's Undisputed and Forged
Letters * Paul's Conflicts with Other Apostles*

The Court:

Good morning, everyone! Ladies and gentlemen of the jury, I
trust you all had a good night's rest and are ready to begin
hearing the second day of *Doubt's* testimony.

Counselor, are you ready to proceed?

Defense:

Good morning, Your Honor. Yes, we are prepared to continue
with *Doubt's* Testimony.

The Court:

Doubt, please take the witness stand. You do realize you are still under oath?

Doubt:

Yes, I do.

Defense:

Good morning, *Doubt*. Are you feeling refreshed and ready to pick up where we left off yesterday afternoon?

Doubt:

I'm looking forward to it!

Defense:

Okay, then. When we recessed yesterday afternoon, we said we were going to talk about problematic passages from other books in the New Testament. Is there a book in particular that you want to look at?

Doubt:

I'd like to look at a colon, sir.

Defense:

I'm sorry, *Doubt*, did you just say you want to open this morning's testimony by talking about a colon?

Doubt:

Yep, I'd like to begin by talking about a colon.

The Court:

Doubt, if you're trying to be funny, I'm here to tell you it's too early in the morning to start making jokes. You are not going to win over the good graces of the jury, and I promise you are not going to amuse me!

Doubt:

It's no joke, Your Honor, and I'm not trying to be funny.

Oh, wait. Are you thinking I want to talk about an organ in the body – the colon?

The Court:

What other kind of colon is there?

Doubt:

The colon; what we all learned in school. The punctuation mark that's two dots, one above the other. You know, the colon.

The Court:

My apologies, *Doubt*. It's just with your reputation and some of your remarks yesterday, I didn't know what to expect. I have no problem with you talking about the punctuation mark, the colon.

Doubt:

Thank you, Your Honor. I'm sorry if my reputation precedes me.

Before talking about the particular colon I want to discuss, I first need to talk about what is shared in a lot of churches in the weeks leading up to Christmas. Some denominations call this time in the Christian calendar Advent. There's a passage in all three synoptic Gospels that's usually read in church services. Although this passage is in all three Gospels, churches pick just one Gospel to read it from. I mentioned the passage yesterday, but for a different reason. This morning, I'd like to point out

125

something about it that's so subtle, unless you're looking for it, you'll read right past it.

Right after the birth narratives in Matthew's and Luke's Gospels, and at the start of Mark's Gospel, we read of John the Baptist quoting the prophet Isaiah. I'm going to recite what the Gospels quote John as saying, but without any punctuation; in other words, I'm going to read through the quote not pausing or doing anything other than reading the words. Here it is as we have it in the Gospels but *without punctuation*:

> "The voice of one crying out in the wilderness prepare the way of the Lord make his paths straight."

John the Baptist is quoting the prophet Isaiah, referring to the fortieth chapter of the Book of Isaiah in the Old Testament. While it's not exactly what Isaiah says, I think it's only fair to give John some slack – after all, about seven hundred years had passed between the time Isaiah said it and when John the Baptist quoted it. Here is the quote, directly from the Book of Isaiah, chapter 40, verse 3:

> "A voice cries out: In the wilderness prepare the way of the Lord, make straight in the desert a highway for our God."

I don't think anyone would disagree that what's in the Book of Isaiah and what John the Baptist says in the Gospels are substantially the same thing.

Now, let's go back to the synoptic Gospels, which use the quote to begin the ministry of Jesus. In all three Gospels, John the Baptist quotes the prophet Isaiah before baptizing Jesus, and then Jesus begins his ministry. In each of the Gospels, here is how it's written *with punctuation*:

> "The voice of one crying out in the wilderness: Prepare the way of the Lord, make his paths straight."

126

Did you pick it up?

Notice where the colon is placed. In the Book of Isaiah in the Old Testament, the colon comes after *a voice cries out*, but in the Gospels, the colon appears after *in the wilderness*. Now does its significance become apparent? The writer of the Book of Isaiah places the colon so the sentence reads that a voice is crying out, and that voice is saying, "In the wilderness prepare the way of the Lord." However, the Gospels place the colon so the sentence reads that a voice *of someone* is crying out in the wilderness, and that voice is saying, "Prepare the way of the Lord."

What the writers of the Gospels have done is to take a quote – a prophecy – from the Old Testament, and change the context of it to fit the person of John the Baptist. You see, John the Baptist was a weird guy who lived in the woods, wore clothing made of camel's hair, and had a diet consisting of locusts and wild honey. He would definitely have been seen as a person in the wilderness. And since he was an itinerant preacher emphatically proclaiming the baptism of repentance, he also would have been seen as a voice crying out.

No matter that the colon has been moved to make the quote fit John the Baptist, thereby fulfilling the prophecy of Isaiah, this passage is used every year to show that Jesus' life was the fulfillment of a prophecy from the Old Testament. This is an annual tradition that is used to prove the divinity of Jesus. Unfortunately, it's not an accurate use of a Bible passage. And even though it's there in plain sight, there's never been a discussion about it in the Church.

Defense:

Why do you think that is, *Doubt*, if you have an opinion on it?

127

Doubt:

Well, you know what they say about opinions!

If I had to point out the obvious, it would be that *a whole lot* of Bibles would have to be edited. And I should point out that it's not just the synoptic Gospels that move the colon to make it fit John the Baptist. In the first chapter of John's Gospel, John the Baptist himself says he is the voice crying out in the wilderness, as said by the prophet Isaiah.

So all four Gospels have the passage from Isaiah fitting John the Baptist. Maybe because there were no proofreaders when the Gospels were written, the movement of the colon could have been a mistake that no one caught.

I'm not sure if I mentioned it yesterday, but we need to remember that Mark's Gospel was written first, at least a decade before Matthew's Gospel; Matthew's Gospel was written maybe five years before Luke's Gospel; and Luke's Gospel was written about a decade before John's Gospel. While it's never been formally identified, the writer of Mark's Gospel used an unknown source for his information; the writer of Matthew's Gospel used 80 to 90 percent of Mark's Gospel as a source; the writer of Luke's Gospel used about 50 percent of Mark's Gospel as a source; and the writer of John's Gospel used mostly unknown sources. So it's possible that the source used by the writer of Mark's Gospel got it wrong – either by accident or intentionally. And then, once Mark's Gospel starting circulating, the writers of Matthew's and Luke's Gospels copied the same mistake. Then the writer of John's Gospel took what was by then the tradition and used it the same way.

Again, this is only my opinion; it's not offered as a matter of factual information.

The Court:

Members of the jury: I've allowed *Doubt* to share his opinion with you. But you are not to use it when considering the verdict. *Doubt's* opinion on why the Church hasn't acted on what he testified to can only be used for your personal consideration after this trial has concluded.

Defense:

Thank you, Your Honor.

Doubt, what else can you tell the jury about some of the books of the Bible?

Doubt:

Well, going back to what's probable or plausible, there is a passage in Matthew's Gospel that might freak out some people. In chapter 27 of Matthew's Gospel, we're told that Jesus breathed his last breath, the Temple curtain was torn in two, and there was a great earthquake causing rocks to split. So far, nothing outrageous, right? Here are the next two verses after that: "The tombs also were opened, and many bodies of the saints who had fallen asleep were raised. After his resurrection they came out of the tombs and entered the city and appeared to many."

I know there are people who enjoy thriller movies, and a zombie apocalypse might be something they might enjoy watching. And there's a popular TV show portraying the dead coming back to life as zombies. But these shows aren't based on reality, and I don't think anyone watching them believes they're real or that they're based on history. Matthew's Gospel writer says numerous dead bodies, that were buried in tombs, came back to life; and when Jesus was resurrected, they strolled the city of Jerusalem. If the members of the jury are going to be instructed to consider testimony and evidence that is more probable than not, I hope they truly think about the probability of dead corpses coming back to life and then walking around a city.

This is another example of a Gospel passage where one needs to consider the message and lesson instead of accepting it as being literally true. The city of Jerusalem was a busy city and only a small percentage of its residents converted to Christianity in the first couple of years after Jesus' death. If dead corpses were walking around the city after the Resurrection of Jesus, it seems to reason that Jewish historians would have been aware of it and documented it. There is no mention of anything like this outside Matthew's Gospel.

Defense:

That's a passage you don't hear that often in church!

Doubt:

Yeah, I wouldn't want to be the preacher who was asked to give a sermon on this passage! In fact, this passage isn't in the calendar used by many of the mainstream Christian denominations. These denominations and churches use a three-year rotating calendar of passages from the Old and New Testaments that are read each week in worship services. I don't think it's by accident that this passage isn't in the calendar.

Defense:

I understand.

What about other issues with what's in the New Testament?

Doubt:

You mean like, who were the disciples?

Defense:

Okay, who were the disciples?

Doubt:

> If you're asking me what their names were, I can't give you an answer that I would trust to be accurate.

Defense:

> Well, *Doubt*, no one can blame you for not knowing every verse or every name in the Bible. I mean, it's not as important to remember every name as it is the message in the passages – isn't that what you've been saying?

Doubt:

> I sure have. But for those who insist the Bible is inerrant and contains the word of God in an infallible way, the question usually causes problems.

Defense:

> Because they can't remember their names either?

Doubt:

> Not necessarily. It's more because there is no way to say with certainty who the disciples were. That is, the names of each of them.

Defense:

> That sounds crazy! Everyone knows there were twelve disciples and each of them had a name. So where's the problem?

Doubt:

> The problem is they have different names in different Gospels.

Defense:

> C'mon, *Doubt*, that can't be right!

131

Doubt:

> All a reader has to do to see that I'm right is find the passages in the New Testament where they name the disciples, then place them side by side and compare the names of the disciples.

> There are four passages in the New Testament that give us the names of the disciples: the three synoptic Gospels and the Book of Acts. John's Gospel doesn't list the disciples' names and many of the names in the passages that do list them never appear in John's Gospel. Most of the names line up exactly in the passages that list them, but there is a name here and there that is different. I'm not going to bore the members of the jury with the lists; if they want to look them up when they have a chance, the list of the names of the disciples can be found in Matthew, Mark, Luke, and the Book of Acts. Specifically, they should look at Matthew 10:2-4; Mark 3:16-19; Luke 6:13-16; and Acts 1:13.

Defense:

> I'm sure some of the members will consider this on their own.

Doubt:

> If they're going to look into that, they might want to consider something else about the disciples.

Defense:

> What's that?

Doubt:

> The number of disciples who were alive when Jesus first appeared to them after his resurrection. Let me explain.

> Collectively, the disciples were known as "the Twelve." Whenever they were talked about as a group in the Gospels and in the other books of the New Testament, they were

132

referred to as the Twelve. Since there were twelve of them, it made sense to call them the Twelve. This is what the writers of the Gospels called them, as did writers of other books. And it would be one of the Twelve who was to betray Jesus so the authorities could arrest him, and ultimately crucify him. I don't think someone needs to be a Christian to know the name Judas. That name is synonymous with betrayal in cultures around the world.

That Judas betrayed Jesus is written in every Gospel. All four Gospels tell how Judas betrayed Jesus on the night he was arrested. One could argue that Judas played a central role in Jesus' arrest, and if not for his betrayal, the story might not have unfolded the way it's documented. If Jesus wasn't arrested that night, his trial and, ultimately, his execution would not have lined up with the Passover.

All four Gospels tell us Jesus predicted his betrayal; in fact, Jesus says his betrayal will fulfill the scripture – to fulfill a prophecy from the Old Testament. Again, the act of betrayal by Judas is a central theme – the central theme – in Jesus' arrest. That arrest led to his prosecution, then to his death.

We're also told in Matthew's Gospel and in the Book of Acts that after he betrayed Jesus, Judas died. Matthew's Gospel says he went out and hanged himself; the Book of Acts says he fell into a field and his body ruptured. While this is certainly a contradiction, I'm not bringing it up for that reason. I'm bringing it up to show that after he betrayed Jesus, Judas died that same night.

In the Book of Acts, we're told that Jesus was with his disciples for forty days before he ascended to Heaven. Right after the ascension, the disciples chose a new disciple to replace Judas, who was dead. In order to have twelve disciples again, they needed to choose someone to replace Judas. A man named Matthias was chosen to replace Judas. We don't know anything

133

about Matthias other than he was a devoted follower of Jesus from his baptism to his resurrection. What's important here isn't the man, Matthias, but to understand that he was chosen forty days after the Resurrection of Jesus. Forty days had passed from Jesus' Crucifixion to the selection of Matthias.

The Court:

Where are you going with this, *Doubt?*

Doubt:

I'm getting there, Your Honor. Just give me a minute.

The Court:

Sixty more seconds to make this all make sense.

Doubt:

Okay, I'll talk fast.

If you recall my testimony from yesterday, I shared that Paul was the earliest Christian writer. His first letter was about twenty years after the death of Jesus, and he continued writing for another ten years or so. So Paul would have had the earliest access to information on what had occurred when Jesus was put to death and his resurrection, right?

In Paul's first letter to the Church in Corinth, he describes the account of Jesus' first appearance after his resurrection. In the fifteenth chapter of that first letter to the Corinthians, Paul says this:

> "For I hand to you as of first importance what I in turn had received: that Christ died for our sins in accordance with the scriptures, and that he was buried, and that he was raised on the third day in accordance with the scriptures, and that he appeared to Cephas, then to the twelve."

It's important to note there that Cephas is Peter; in John's Gospel, when he was calling his first disciples, Jesus gave him the name Cephas, which means Peter. So at the Resurrection, Jesus first appeared to Peter, and then to the Twelve.

Do you see that? Jesus appeared to *the Twelve*!

Defense:

I don't understand the significance of this, *Doubt*. Didn't you say that Jesus' disciples were known as the Twelve? What's the issue here?

Doubt:

The issue is a problem with the number of disciples!

How could there be twelve disciples – the Twelve – if Judas was dead? Only eleven of Jesus' disciples were alive after the Crucifixion. Matthias wasn't added to the eleven until forty days later, so there couldn't have been twelve disciples that Jesus appeared to. Jesus could not have appeared to the Twelve. Instead, he would have appeared to eleven disciples.

One thing to keep in mind is that Paul was writing about what he had been told. He was writing about the information that was available to him at the time of his letters. So one thing to consider is that during the time of his writing this first letter to the folks in Corinth, the tradition circulating among the early Christians seems to have been that Judas played no significant role in Jesus' death, and that he was still alive at the Resurrection. This consideration is further bolstered by the fact that even though Paul talks about Jesus being betrayed, he never says who betrayed him – Paul never mentions Judas by name.

This is unusual for Paul, not going into further detail when he brings up a topic, because his letters are filled with details and he doesn't seem to have a problem naming those who are

135

against the Way of Jesus. But here in this letter, Paul doesn't even seem to know a disciple named Judas. Consider that the betrayal of Jesus was seen as being the worst thing that a disciple could have done to him; why, then, would Paul mention the betrayal but omit the name of the betrayer?

In this passage, Paul was talking about the disciples as if they were still the Twelve that are mentioned throughout the New Testament – they were still together as the original twelve disciples. If that's the case, and it sure seems to be here, that must have been the understanding of what happened at the time he wrote this letter. Scholars believe this is one of Paul's earliest letters, probably written around year 51 of the Common Era.

Here's one way to think about it: When someone mentions the rock band, The Fab Four, what do you think about? Anyone who knows anything about classic rock knows that the Beatles were referred to as "The Fab Four." They became known around the world as The Fab Four. But what if one of their members had died while they were still together – would they still have been called The Fab Four? Of course not. It wouldn't have made sense to call a band with now only three members The Fab Four. Even now, the term "The Fab Four" is only used when referring to the band when it was complete, before their breakup decades ago. In the same way, it wouldn't have made sense for the apostle Paul to refer to the disciples as the Twelve, unless the information he had at the time said all twelve of the original disciples were still alive. So were the accounts of Judas being dead just wrong? We'll probably never know.

One additional passage regarding the original twelve disciples at the time of the Resurrection can be found in a gospel that didn't make it into the New Testament, but at its time, it was considered authoritative. The Gospel of Peter was written in a timeframe somewhere before Mark's Gospel was written and after the last book of the New Testament was written – a span of more than fifty years! Most scholars place it being written in the early part of the second century while a few others believe it was written before the fall of Jerusalem in the year 70 of the Common Era. That's a big window, for sure.

Even though the approximate year it was written can't be established as narrowly as the Gospels that made their way into the New Testament, that doesn't mean people who read it didn't believe it. Regardless of when it was written, there's a passage in Peter's Gospel that describes what happened after the death of Jesus. It reads like this: "But we twelve disciples of the Lord were weeping and sorrowful; and each one, sorrowful because of what had come to pass, departed to his home."

It needs to be noted that Peter's Gospel is harsh toward the Jewish authorities and paints them in a less than favorable way. And the writer of it makes no bones in directly accusing the Jews of crucifying Jesus. Whoever the writer of Peter's Gospel was, he would certainly take no pity in naming the one who betrayed Jesus and ultimately caused his death. And yet, like the writings of Paul, he never singles out Judas as the one who betrayed Jesus. It's as if Judas was just another one of the Twelve.

Defense:

I read right past that passage in the Book of Acts without even thinking about it that way. I'm amazed at how easy it is for the casual reader of the New Testament to miss these problematic passages.

Doubt:

Easy for the casual reader to miss, but not for biblical scholars. This one passage alone has caused debate for centuries among scholars and theologians. Some of them find ways to explain the discrepancy and others point out that it can't be explained away. And this passage isn't the only one they debate about regarding Judas.

Defense:

What do you mean?

Doubt:

As I said just a few minutes ago, there are two accounts of how Judas died – one in Matthew's Gospel and the other in the Book of Acts. Also, there are two additional accounts of how he died in books that didn't make it into the New Testament, and those accounts are different from those in the New Testament. Debates and discussions have gone on for centuries regarding this issue, as those who want to stick with their belief that the Bible is without errors claim the contradiction can be explained and those on the other side point out that it can't be explained away.

And finally, there's one more issue with Judas, but it doesn't come from the Bible. It comes from the Book of Tobit in the Old Testament of Catholic and Orthodox Bibles, and is a well-known mythical story that had been circulating in that part of the world for hundreds of years before the death of Jesus. It's *The Story of Ahikar*, also known as the *Words of Ahikar*.

The principal character, Ahikar, is a very wise man who adopts his nephew, Nadan. Ahikar trains Nadan in his wisdom. But the reward for this sharing of wisdom to Nadan is that Nadan betrays Ahikar with false allegations that lead to a death sentence for Ahikar. Fortunately for Ahikar, his life is spared at the last minute, but that wasn't known to Nadan, who believed his uncle was dead. When Nadan heard his uncle giving a speech some days later, Nadan "swelled up and became like a blown-out bladder. And his limbs swelled and his legs and his feet and his side, and he was torn and his belly

138

burst asunder and his entrails were scattered, and he perished, and died."

Obviously, this is just a short synopsis of the story – a *very short* synopsis. I don't think it's necessary to go into the details of the story. But I do think it's important to share with the members of the jury that some biblical scholars and theologians believe there are too many parallels between this story's character, Nadan, and the story of Judas' betrayal and his death for it to be a coincidence. They believe the story of Judas was taken from this and other tales being shared in that part of the world. This parallel story, when added to the discrepancies already discussed, gives those who question the details of the betrayal of Jesus and the death of Judas understandable reasons for their theories. However, there are just as many – probably more – scholars who believe Jesus was betrayed and his betrayer was Judas.

Defense:

Are you suggesting we don't believe the entire story of Judas? Are you saying he never existed?

Doubt:

No, not at all!

It bears repeating again: My purpose in life *is not* to make people believe or disbelieve anything; instead, it's to create that feeling that pushes a person to dig deeper, to look further than what's obvious. What anyone takes away from the information I just shared about Judas is as personal as each member of the jury sitting here today. I'm not the one to say what should be done with this new information. My job here today is to present it and let the jury decide what to make of it.

Defense:

I'm glad you keep reminding us of that, *Doubt.* I can see how, without this reminder, some people might see you as a troublemaker trying to stir things up just to get someone to change their beliefs.

Doubt:

Thanks. It's a never-ending battle. What most people don't understand about me is that I honor their beliefs, I honor their thoughts and, when it comes to religion, I honor their faith. My hope is that there will come a time when people themselves can develop an understanding that they can honor their thoughts, beliefs, and faith while still finding room for me in their lives.

That being said, how about I throw something out there that I just remembered that might stretch the comfort zone of those who firmly believe in the physical resurrection of Jesus?

Defense:

If you think this is a good time to share it with the jury, sure.

Doubt:

I'm sorry if it seems I'm bouncing all over the place. It's just there are times, as I'm sitting here sharing what I know, when I think of something that I believe is important for the members of the jury to hear. And I don't want to blurt them out because that might upset the judge.

The Court:

And I do appreciate that, *Doubt.*

Doubt:

So when they pop into my head, I make a mental note and then come back to them when I'm finished with my previous train of thought. And they're all stored in my head; it's not like I've had the time to sit down and write them down in a book.

Defense:

We understand, *Doubt.* Now, you were saying you had something to share about the Resurrection.

Doubt:

I think this will be a good segue into what I'd like to talk about next. So here goes.

We've established that Paul was a very detailed writer whose letters are the earliest texts we have in the New Testament. He was also a very passionate man who appeared to wear his heart on his sleeve. While Paul claimed most of his knowledge and wisdom came from visions he had where God and Jesus visited him, he also gained some of his knowledge from the people he spoke with. He wrote about what was known to have been circulating at the time; scholars refer to this as what the traditions were at the time. And that only makes sense, right?

Paul, in conversations with the apostles and other followers of Jesus, learned about Jesus and his ministry, as well as the events of his death and resurrection. It's important to remember here that Paul never met Jesus; Paul's conversion to Christianity was anywhere between one and six years after Jesus was crucified. Still, even though he never met Jesus, that didn't stop Paul from writing letters to numerous communities and people giving his interpretation of Jesus' teachings.

Which brings me to the Resurrection. As I said earlier, Paul talks about the betrayal of Jesus, but he doesn't name the betrayer; in fact, it seems as if Paul never heard of Judas. The same can be said of the empty tomb. The earliest writer of the New Testament never once mentioned the empty tomb in all those early letters.

Paul talks about Jesus' resurrection often in his letters. He talks about him dying on the cross. However, he never once mentions the empty tomb in any of his letters. This well-educated and articulate man routinely gave detailed accounts of his own experiences as well as detailed descriptions of others and their actions. If this is the case, as is in the case with omitting Judas' name, why would he fail to talk about the tomb that was found empty on that Sunday morning that has become known as Easter?

According to Roman tradition, Jesus' body should have been left hanging on the cross for days after he was dead. In a close-to-miraculous way, it was carried to a tomb by a wealthy man who up until that point in the Gospels, no one had heard of. You see, when the Romans crucified criminals, part of that punishment was what happened after they died on the cross. The humiliation of a loved one's naked dead body hanging on the cross for days afterwards was meant to send a message and act as a deterrent. Scavengers – wild dogs and birds – would eat at the rotting bodies before they were removed after some days and dumped in a communal grave outside the city. But that didn't happen to Jesus. In a never before act of compassion, Pontius Pilate allowed his body to be taken down from the cross right after he died.

A rich man, Joseph of Arimathea, carried Jesus to a tomb he had bought and made sure he was given a proper burial. A large stone was placed in front of the tomb to prevent Jesus' body from being disturbed or, worse yet, stolen. Although they differ in a number of places, all four Gospels say some of Jesus' followers went to the tomb the third morning after his death. When they arrived there, they found the stone rolled away and Jesus' body gone. Then, depending on which Gospel account you read, these visitors to the tomb were greeted by one or more angelic beings telling them Jesus wasn't there.

The empty tomb is synonymous with Easter morning in every Christian denomination around the world. The symbolism itself is moving and its importance was known by the time the first Gospel, Mark, was written. Otherwise, the writer wouldn't have included it. So why did Paul fail to include it? Is it possible he never heard of it?

Biblical scholars believe it is because Paul had never heard of the tradition of the empty tomb; if he had heard of it, he most certainly would have mentioned it. This means, according to them, the tradition of the empty tomb was a "post-Pauline tradition," meaning it came about after Paul was done writing his letters. This is not to say that Jesus wasn't crucified, nor does it deny the Resurrection. Scholars say Paul's omission of the empty tomb in his letters only points to the argument that Paul never heard of it. It's the theologians and members of the clergy who argue that this either proves or disproves anything.

Defense:

To summarize your last two points regarding Paul, what you're saying is that if Paul had heard that Judas was the one who betrayed Jesus, and if Paul had heard of the empty tomb, he would have made note of them in his letters. Is that your testimony?

Doubt:

Yes, it is.

Defense:

Thank you.

Doubt, you said you wanted to use your last bit of testimony as a segue. What do you want to segue into?

143

Doubt:

The apostle Paul. I've mentioned him numerous times, but never went into any depth about his ministry or anything about him. I'd like to do that now, if that's okay?

Defense:

I'm sure the jury would like to learn more about him. Go ahead.

Doubt:

Okay, first a little bit about Paul. Paul was born in a town called Tarsus in Turkey; for this reason, Paul was originally called Paul of Tarsus. Actually, he was called Saul of Tarsus; Paul is the Greek name for Saul. Paul gained a reputation in the area around Jerusalem as a persecutor of the early Christians. However, one day while traveling to Damascus, he was blinded by a great light and Jesus spoke to him. Paul was asked by Jesus, "Saul, Saul, why do you persecute me?"

Paul was blind for three days and was led to Damascus by two men who were traveling with him. While in Damascus, another man was instructed by the Lord to lay his hands on Paul. When he did this, Paul's vision was restored. Paul was then baptized and began to proclaim Jesus' name in the synagogues. This has become known as the conversion of Saul.

Paul believed God wanted him to make it his life's mission to convert people to Christianity for their salvation. So his ministry was converting people throughout the land. As he went from town to town, he would start churches with the people he converted. After some time passed, after planting churches, word would occasionally get back to him that there was a problem in a certain church, and the church leaders would ask for his advice. The letters that form all but a couple of the books that bear his name in the New Testament are his responses to those leaders. The other letters are to individuals.

144

With that as a background, here are some things to keep in mind regarding Paul. Some people – most people for that matter – are surprised to learn that there is almost nothing in Paul's letters that have the words, teachings, or actions of Jesus. Because of this, there are names given to what he preached: Pauline Christianity and Pauline Theology. Some biblical scholars and theologians have argued against Paul's teachings because they are not from Jesus. Remember, Paul never met Jesus.

Since Paul never met Jesus, one might ask how he gained his knowledge or understanding of Jesus' message. Paul said he received all his knowledge through revelations with God and Jesus. Paul claimed that God and Jesus spoke to him in visions and the information he received from them was to be considered authoritative as having come from God or Jesus themselves. In fact, the Christian Eucharist liturgies in almost every denomination and church are from Paul's first letter to the church in Corinth – *First Corinthians* as it's called in the New Testament. The Words of Institution, also called the Words of Consecration, are told by Paul in that letter. But how did Paul know what those familiar words were? Paul says he received those words from the Lord.

Paul's letters have influenced just about every aspect of Christianity, including baptism and the concept of Heaven and hell. When I say Paul's letters, I am referring to the letters that are ascribed to him in the New Testament – that is, the letters that bear his name. I believe I mentioned yesterday that of the thirteen letters signed by Paul, only seven are universally considered to be authentic. The other six letters are called the disputed letters

> *Paul preached that one cannot be justified through works; a person can only be justified by their faith in Jesus. James claimed that faith without works is dead; he said we are justified through our works.*

145

from Paul. Scholars can't agree on whether all six of them are forgeries, but they do agree that at least four of them are forgeries. Someone other than Paul wrote these disputed letters and signed Paul's name to them.

It was not unusual for Paul to get into disagreements with people. And one of those people was none other than Jesus' brother, James. In fact, they didn't care for each other. At the heart of their disagreements was the idea of becoming justified with God; that is, becoming right with God again. Paul preached that one cannot be justified through works; a person can only be justified by their faith in Jesus. James claimed that faith without works is dead; he said we are justified through our works.

James wasn't the only one who Paul had a problem with. There was an incident that Paul wrote about saying he called out Peter to his face. And in the Book of Acts, there's a documented problem between Paul and Barnabas. Many scholars and theologians, as well as clergy and laypeople familiar with his works, acknowledge that Paul had a rather large self-image. This is one reason why some say Paul wrote his own Gospel according to his beliefs.

Also noteworthy for our discussion is the writer of Luke's Gospel and the Book of Acts. It's widely held throughout the academic communities that he is the same person – the person who wrote Luke's Gospel also wrote the Book of Acts. And it's also known that Luke was a companion of Paul. So it would make sense that Luke held Paul in some esteem. This might explain why roughly 50 percent – one half – of the Book of Acts is devoted to Paul and what he did in his ministry. When one considers there were twelve other apostles (the original disciples plus Matthias and excluding Judas), it's interesting that half of the one book devoted to their acts after the death of Jesus is focused on Paul. The Book of Acts is supposed to narrate the acts of the apostles – all the apostles. Instead, only a handful are followed, and of those, the focus is on Paul.

I want the jury to know that I'm not bringing these things up to unfairly put Paul down. I'm bringing them up because they usually aren't discussed in Bible study and I think it's important for people to know what is discussed in seminaries and theological schools around the world.

Defense:

And I'm sure the members of the jury appreciate that, *Doubt*.

I think we can move on to some other concerns now. However, maybe Your Honor would like to take a break before we get started on another topic. Instead of interrupting *Doubt's* testimony partially through his testimony on a specific issue, maybe it would be best to stop here and give the jury a chance to stretch their legs and grab a drink and snack.

The Court:

Counselor, that sounds like a great idea. My legs could use a good stretch as well!

Chapter 8:

Midmorning Testimony, Day 2

Paul's Second Letter to the Corinthians * More Problematic Passages * A Cross to Bear * Day of Jesus' Death in John's Gospel * Symbolism in the Minds of the Gospel Writers * Reading Each Gospel as Its Own Book * New Testament Information Writers Would Not Have Had Access To * Passages from the Book of Acts * How Many Gods? * Is There More Than One God According to the Trinity?

The Court:

Welcome back, everyone.

Counselor, you may proceed with your client's testimony.

Defense:

Thank you, Judge.

Doubt, before we took our morning break, you had just completed your testimony about Paul and were prepared to move on to some other concerns. What are some of those concerns, as you call them?

Doubt:

I know I keep doing this, but can I go back to Paul for just one quick point? I think the jury will find it interesting.

Defense:

One quick point, *Doubt*, sure.

Doubt:

Thank you. I'll make it as a fast as I can.

If you remember from before the break, I talked about the undisputed letters from Paul, and how there are seven of them. Out of the thirteen letters he wrote, scholars are just about unanimous in agreeing that seven were definitely from Paul himself. But what critical scholars also are in agreement on is an issue with Paul's second letter to the church in Corinth. This letter is known as Second Corinthians.

Here is what is taught in universities around the world and has been for more than 100 years: Paul did not write Second Corinthians. Second Corinthians is made up of at least two letters from Paul that were combined into one book – chapters 10 through 13 don't come from the same letter as chapters 1 through 9. Biblical scholars believe there were at least two letters from Paul that were circulating after Paul's first letter to the Corinthians; letters that were copied – and changed. They were circulating until someone took both and combined them into one letter, giving it the name *Second Corinthians*. So that's how Second Corinthians came to be – by taking parts of the two letters and splicing them together.

It's important to note that in the last fifty years, some biblical scholars believe there were at least five different letters from Paul circulating that were combined, not just two. Five different letters from Paul were gathered together, selected passages copied, then put into one letter to create Second

149

Corinthians. Kind of like an early attempt at cutting and pasting text from different documents to make one you're happy with.

It's also important to share that scholars have good evidence from the New Testament that Paul dictated his letters to scribes. And we've already discussed the mistakes scribes made in other books of the Bible. I'm not saying every one of the undisputed letters from Paul had mistakes, but it stands to reason that there were mistakes.

Defense:

Fascinating, *Doubt*. Now we can move on to some other concerns. What are they?

Doubt:

There are several passages, as I've said numerous times in this trial, that are problematic for various reasons and to various people. Obviously, we can't go through each page of the Bible pointing out where a problem or contradiction might be found, so I'd like to briefly mention just a few. They aren't ranked in any way as one being any more problematic than another, nor am I selecting what I think are the most troublesome. I'm just going to randomly pick a few to show some variety in my testimony. Everyone likes variety, right?

The Court:

Doubt.

Doubt:

Sorry, Your Honor. Gotta stay on track. I understand.

Maybe it's best to start off with a saying most people have heard at some point in their life. You don't have to be a Christian to have heard it. It goes something like this: "We all have a cross to bear." This saying comes from the time of

Jesus. It alludes to Jesus' Crucifixion when he was made to carry his own cross to the site of the Crucifixion.

This saying is closely related to passages found in all three synoptic Gospels, and these passages are often shared among Christians in discussions and sometimes, perhaps, even as words of encouragement. The quote in these passages differ slightly in wording, but the message is the same: Jesus says if anyone wants to be one of his followers, they must deny themselves and take up their cross and follow him. He also says in other chapters of these Gospels something very similar: that whoever does not carry their cross and follow him cannot be one of his disciples.

Certainly, on the surface, there doesn't seem to be anything disconcerting about this passage, I agree. This message, this passage about picking up our cross and following Jesus, evokes so many different emotions. For some, it's a wake-up call of sorts – a motivational message to stop complaining about life and to instead follow the teachings of Jesus. For others, it brings back the image of Jesus carrying his cross to the site of his execution, or that of a passerby who was ordered by the Roman soldiers to carry Jesus' cross. Carrying one's cross and following Jesus is seen as a righteous and honorable thing to do.

That image of the cross – one can only imagine what it meant to the Jewish people of that day. While we can't interview any of them two thousand years later, we do have some historical references to what the cross meant to the Jewish community. It was a sign of hatred, a symbol of torture and humiliation. Up until the time Jesus was crucified on a cross, the image of a cross brought nothing but fear to all those who lived at that time.

What a wonderful turnaround humankind has made: It's taken a symbol of hatred, fear, and humiliation and turned it into a message of hope and love. And if not for the death of Jesus on it, it's unlikely we would even give it a second thought today. It would have probably faded into history as the Romans came up with new, more efficient ways to execute criminals. Time has a way of letting go of the past, doesn't it?

I would imagine that if we were all Jews living in early first-century Palestine right now, a time before Jesus began his ministry, we wouldn't give much thought to a cross unless we happened to be passing by the site where criminals were crucified. We wouldn't use it as a metaphor for anything, simply because of what it represented. I would compare it to a noose in a community of color. If we were all people of color, living in a predominately black community, we wouldn't see the noose as anything other than a symbol of hate and horrible acts committed in our history. None of us would even think about wearing a small noose as a necklace! That would be unthinkable. I know that's a very harsh comparison. I wish I could think of something else, but that's the one that came to mind. Maybe in today's time it would be like wearing a symbol of the electric chair around our necks; it just wouldn't make any sense.

Going back to the time of Jesus: Jesus is quoted in all three synoptic Gospels as telling people if they want to be his followers, they need to pick up their cross and follow him. Here's the problem: The cross did not have any religious significance for the followers of Jesus until after his Crucifixion. Telling someone to pick up their cross would be more than confusing for anyone to hear because there was no meaning to it. The significance of the cross, and carrying one's cross, came *after* the Crucifixion of Jesus.

Up until the time of the Crucifixion, the cross had that fearful, hate-filled connotation. After the Crucifixion, and Jesus' subsequent resurrection, his followers gained courage and resolve. As the Way of Jesus spread, so did the stories of his courage. By the time the first Gospel was written, the followers of Jesus used the cross for a different purpose than what it was designed for. They regarded it in a different light – so the cross became a symbol of resurrection and eternal life, rather than death.

The question scholars ask is: Why would Jesus mention the cross with those words found in the passages in the Gospels? While there is nothing funny about it, an analogy might be to a callback a comedian uses in a standup routine. In terms of a comedy routine, a callback is a joke that refers to a joke told earlier in the routine. The second joke refers to the first joke to make it work. If the first joke wasn't told, the second joke has no meaning, so the audience doesn't get it. With the passages where Jesus tells his followers to pick up their cross and follow him, there had to first be a significant meaning to the cross in order for them to get what Jesus was saying. For this reason, biblical scholars and historians, including the members of the Jesus Seminar, question whether this is something Jesus actually said or if it's a quote simply ascribed to him by the earliest writer of the Gospels – that is, by the author of Mark's Gospel.

Defense:

So what you're saying, *Doubt*, is that the cross would have no significant Christian meaning before Jesus was crucified on it? Therefore, the passages that contain his quotes about it are found questionable by scholars?

Doubt:

Yes. That's not to say that he couldn't have said what's recorded in those passages. But they're quotes that wouldn't have had any meaning unless Jesus had already been crucified on the cross. I should add, again, that Mark's Gospel was the first Gospel written and the writers of Matthew's and Luke's Gospels used Mark's Gospel as their primary source, so they would have seen these passages and copied them into their Gospels. That's probably why the passages are in all three synoptic Gospels.

Defense:

That makes sense, doesn't it? If Mark's Gospel was written first, the writers of the other two synoptic Gospels would have had access to Mark's work.

Doubt:

That's what the people who spend their waking hours studying this stuff say.

Defense:

What else can you share with the members of the jury?

Doubt:

I think the jury might be interested in hearing more about Jesus' arrest, so I'd like to mention something there.

We just talked about the synoptic Gospels, and how Matthew's and Luke's Gospels used Mark's Gospel as a source. The writer of John's Gospel would have definitely known about the first three Gospels written, but for reasons we touched on earlier, he appears to have chosen to use very little of them for his Gospel. Now, I'd like to point out something that shines a light on the difference between the three synoptic Gospels and John's Gospel. It's an event, the same event, documented in all four Gospels. But this example will show how different John's Gospel, and its portrayal of Jesus, can be. It's the death of Jesus.

Before we get to that, it's important to look a little deeper into how John's Gospel differs from the synoptic Gospels. That difference was known to the early church fathers who saw John's Gospel as a very spiritual Gospel, sharing stories of

Jesus in ways that were symbolically different than the synoptic Gospels. One major difference was the portrayal of Jesus. A central theme in John's Gospel was Jesus as the Lamb of God. This was evident from the first introduction of Jesus in John's Gospel; John the Baptist sees Jesus coming, and he says, "Here is the Lamb of God who takes away the sin of the world!" [John 1:29]

Jesus, the Lamb of God who takes away the sins of the world: This is something just about every Christian has heard at one time or another during their faith journey. And the story of Jesus, as told by the writers of John's Gospel, is bracketed by the theme of the Lamb of God. John's Gospel opens with Jesus being introduced as the Lamb of God, and as we'll see in a minute, Jesus' life ends with him being the symbolic sacrificial lamb.

In the three synoptic Gospels, Jesus shares the Passover meal with his disciples; but in John's Gospel, Jesus' last supper is eaten before the beginning of Passover. In the three synoptic Gospels, Jesus is crucified on Passover; in John's Gospel, Jesus is crucified on the Day of Preparation – the day before Passover. Why the different days?

Biblical scholars believe it was to continue the theme of Jesus being the Lamb of God. In those days, Jews would have their lambs sacrificed for the Passover meal. That day was the Day of Preparation, the day before Passover. In John's Gospel, Jesus is crucified the same day the lambs are slaughtered for the Passover meal – the same day they are *sacrificed*.

I've brought this up to show that even when the Gospels aren't historically accurate or in agreement with each other, that doesn't mean the one that's different isn't significant. In Paul's first letter to the Corinthians, he writes: "For our paschal lamb, Christ, has been sacrificed." The Paschal Lamb was the lamb offered as the sacrifice for Passover. One of the themes of

155

John's Gospel is Jesus as the Lamb of God. Jesus died not for his sins, but for the sins of others. His death, in a very real way, was a sacrifice for the sins of others.

This symbolism of Jesus as the Lamb of God has become one of the most overriding themes in the Christian tradition. The image of the Lamb has shown up in Christian art throughout the world, and that symbolism carries on into Christian liturgies such as Communion, where those receiving it might hear that they are receiving the Sacrament in remembrance of Christ's sacrifice for them. And there are hundreds of hymns, if not more, with the theme of Jesus as the Lamb of God.

None of this is to suggest that because his death was documented on different days means he wasn't really crucified. To the contrary, biblical scholars, historians, and anthropologists are almost unanimous in agreeing that the man Jesus was a real person; that he was an itinerant apocalyptic preacher who caused so much trouble that he eventually became a threat to the authorities, so he was sentenced to death; and that death was by crucifixion under the Roman empire. None of this is disputed by reputable scholars.

Defense:

Would this be another one of those subtle differences in the Gospels that if you weren't looking for it, you wouldn't find it?

Doubt:

Exactly. Some people read the New Testament either by thinking about or meditating on a verse; then they go to that book in the New Testament and read it. Others read passages by using what I call the "I'll let God decide what I should read" approach; they grab their Bible and fan the pages until they feel it's the right time to stop – then they read what's on that page. And then there are those who sit down with the intention of reading the New Testament from beginning to end.

156

They read Matthew's Gospel first, then go on to Mark's Gospel, where they realize that a lot of it sounds familiar – in some places, it sounds almost identical to Matthew's Gospel. So naturally they assume it's just about the same. Then, they go on to read Luke's Gospel, and a lot of what they read in Luke's Gospel sounds like what they've already read in the previous two Gospels. Again, they assume everything is lining up with one another. Then when they get to John's Gospel, they either see that it's the same basic story but with more details and lengthy monologues from Jesus, or they recall someone telling them that John's Gospel is different, but the message about Jesus is the same. And since it all seems to be in line, all four Gospels tend to line up in their minds. It's something that happens to just about everyone other than clergy members, seminary professors, and biblical scholars. So if you've found yourself as someone who believed that all four Gospels are aligned perfectly with one another, don't fret!

Remember, each Gospel writer had a theological idea of what they wanted to convey. And they were tasked with the responsibility of painting a picture of Jesus decades after his death – a man they never met and writing in a place he probably had never visited. Scholars and theologians agree that the symbolism of Jesus as the Lamb of God was a significant theological statement about the death of Jesus.

Defense:

Symbolism sure seems to have been an important way to share information in the days of Jesus. Are there other symbolic passages that you want to bring up?

Doubt:

While there are many more symbolisms, I think I made the point I wanted to make about how the different Gospel writers documented the death of Jesus and, in doing so, the message of his ministry became clearer. With that in mind, I'd like to go off on a short tangent. Just a short one, all right, Your Honor?

The Court:

Let's hear it, *Doubt.*

Doubt:

I hope I wasn't rambling earlier when I talked about how people read the New Testament Gospels. I want to take that one step further by mentioning the risk we run if we assume all four are the same. The obvious first thing to point out is there are four of them; if they were all the same, we would only need one Gospel. But we have four; four Gospels written by at least five different men, living at different times and in different places.

What I want to stress is what's taught in seminaries and theological schools: that we should read each Gospel on its own, and we should read it and let it stand on its own merit. We would do the Gospels a disservice as a whole and individually if we were to assume they are all alike. Each writer wrote from his own perspective and from his own experiences in life. And as I said yesterday, each writer had a unique emphasis they wanted to relate as they told the story of Jesus. The writer of Mark's Gospel stressed how Jesus was the new Messiah; the writer of Matthew's Gospel stressed not only that Jesus was the new Messiah, he was also the new Moses; the writer of Luke's Gospel stressed the idea that the good news of Jesus was for the gentiles as much as it was the Jews; and the writers of John's Gospel – remember, most scholars say there were at least two writers – stressed the divinity of Jesus.

With that as a background, consider this: Would any of you, the members of the jury, think that a person who watches Fox News gets the same information as a person who watches only MSNBC, and would a person who listens to Rush Limbaugh

158

on the radio get the same news as someone who listens to NPR? All four of the figurative people in these examples would tell you that they are up on the news of the day. But would it be fair to them, or to their sources of the news, to believe that they got the *right news*? Let's further assume these four people are outspoken in their political beliefs; what would it look and sound like if we put them in a room together?

Another example is to use an analogy of a periodical such as *Reader's Digest*. Imagine if there were four books, the condensed version of them, in your copy of *Reader's Digest*. Let's say the four books were written by authors writing over a course of, oh say, thirty years – the same time span in which the four Gospels of the New Testament were written. The publisher of this copy of *Reader's Digest* wants to show literary works that helped shaped America. The publisher wants people to read them so they better understand what America was like in the second half of the nineteenth century. The books are: *The Scarlet Letter* by Nathaniel Hawthorne; *Little Women* by Louisa May Alcott; *The Adventures of Huckleberry Finn* by Mark Twain; and *The Red Badge of Courage* by Stephen Crane.

All four books are bound together in this *Reader's Digest* that you're holding. Would anyone reading the first book, *The Scarlet Letter*, believe it contained the same story as *The Red Badge of Courage*? Of course not! Each writer wrote about what they believed was important when they put pen to paper. To get an honest picture in our minds, we would need to read each author's book in the spirit in which it was written. We would never think to compare one to another and assume they say the same thing.

Or, take a road atlas for another example – a book of road maps of each state. The purpose of the book is singular: to give drivers instructions on which routes will get them to where they want to go. However, even though each page has a map on it, a person reading it likely would understand that each state

159

map is unique to that state. Let's say a person was bored, and decided they wanted to read a road atlas. The state maps in the atlas would be in alphabetical order. The person would begin with a road map of the state of Alabama; when they were done, they would turn the page to a map of the state of Alaska. Would that person believe the roads in Alabama are the same as the ones in Alaska? Would she or he assume that the roads in the maps in Alaska picked up where the roads in Alabama left off? Of course not.

My point is this: The New Testament didn't fall into the hands of the early church fathers already bound in leather, organized by book, with chapter numbers and verses in them. It developed over the course of hundreds of years with many debates over which books should be included and which ones weren't worthy of being a part of it. The Gospels were written decades apart. To assume they all agreed with one another would be to assume the writers somehow got together and decided each would emphasize a different nature of Jesus.

Defense:

That's one heck of a tangent, *Doubt!*

I wonder how many members of the jury ever thought about the books of the Bible and especially the New Testament in that way.

Doubt:

Not just the members of the jury. I wonder how many people have ever considered this about the Bible – the books of the Bible, and the writers who authored them.

With that in mind, I'd like to continue with an issue that takes what I just shared and shines a different light on it.

Defense:

We'd like to hear that.

Doubt:

We know the writers of all the books in the Bible had their own biases and beliefs, as well as their understandings of what needed to be shared to paint the picture they wanted to share with their readers. I've mentioned that Mark's Gospel was the first to be written and the writer of Mark's Gospel had an unknown source that scholars and historians call "Q." Q stands for the German word *quell*, which means "source" in German. What scholars believe is that the writer of Mark's Gospel had to get his information on what Jesus said and did from somewhere. After all, he was writing about forty years after Jesus' death and he needed a source for his Gospel. Q is a hypothetical collection of Jesus' sayings and his deeds that the writers of the synoptic Gospels used as a source, especially for Mark's Gospel.

Most scholars accept Q as a source, and more recently, other sources have been uncovered, and each of them has been given a letter. The direction I'm going isn't to the sources of the Gospels; I just feel that the information about Q is important as a foundation for where I'm going now. We know that there weren't eyewitnesses to what Jesus said and did; that is, there weren't people who followed him and wrote everything down. Nothing was written down until the Gospels were written between forty and seventy years after Jesus' death. And letters from Paul about the churches being established didn't start to be written until twenty years after Jesus' death.

The issue I want to talk about isn't about the sources in general. It's how some of the passages that are written in the Gospels and in the Book of Acts could be known to anyone other than those involved in each event. For example, if Jesus had a private conversation with Pontius Pilate, as is written in John's

161

Gospel, who was there to record what was said? John's Gospel says Pilate took Jesus into his headquarters and questioned him in private – it specifically says the guards waited outside. Before that, before Jesus was arrested, it is said in all four Gospels that Jesus went away by himself and prayed to the Father – he prayed to God. If Jesus went and prayed privately to God, how could what he said to God be recorded? There are other passages where Jesus or his disciples were away from the conversation being written about, yet their private conversations, and even their thoughts, are written in the passages. How could the writer know what was said, or what someone was thinking, if it was done in private?

As an example, in the seventh chapter of John's Gospel, we're told Jesus was talking to a crowd in an outside area where a festival was going on. The Pharisees and the chief priests send the Temple police to arrest Jesus. On hearing the wisdom of Jesus, the Temple police don't arrest him, but they go back to the Pharisees and chief priest and tell them they didn't arrest him because of his wisdom and the way he spoke. If the Temple police went back to the Pharisees and chief priests, and talked to them away from where the action was happening (that the narrator of the passage is describing), how could anyone know what the Temple police said?

The Book of Acts has this issue throughout its chapters. A few examples are: In the fifth chapter, we're told the Temple police reported back to the council, which was meeting in private, and reported what they saw – or who they didn't see – in a jail cell. If the council was meeting in private, how would it be known what the Temple police told them? Just a few verses later, there's another conversation by different people in the council. Again, if that conversation was held, who would have been there to record it? One more example is in the sixth chapter, where it specifically says that some men were secretly there to

162

instigate, to lie, and to stir up trouble. If this was done in secret, how could anyone know about it to write it down?

These are just some examples that highlight the problem writers have when trying to make sense of the information they have compared to the outcome they need to explain. This isn't to say that what was said in private didn't happen. Rather, it's to point out the problem of how the words or actions done in private, without any witnesses, could have become known to the writers of the Gospels. And I should include the reminder that the person who wrote Luke's Gospel also wrote the Book of Acts. So when I say the writers of the Gospels had a problem, that also includes the writer of the Book of Acts.

> *How could words or actions done in private, without any witnesses, have become known to the writers of the Gospels?*

Defense:

You know, when you read through these books of the New Testament, you don't even think about all the conversations and acts that were done in private; you just assume that there was someone there to record what happened. The way they're written – it's as if you are there, along for the ride, observing everything as it is happening. Yet in reality, the Gospels and the Book of Acts are books written not from a first-person perspective, but instead from the perspective of a reporter who is telling the story decades after it happened.

Doubt:

That's right. And I'll keep repeating myself: I'm not saying these things didn't happen or weren't said. They very well might have. These are simply examples of why I manifest in people who read these books from a critical and historical perspective. Sometimes, I even show up in people who read them from a devotional standpoint – when their critical faculty kicks in and they wonder how this or that could have been known – that's when I usually show up.

Defense:

So you're not saying these conversations and actions didn't happen. Instead, you are questioning how they could have been recorded to be written decades later in the books you mentioned. Is that your testimony?

Doubt:

Yes, in a nutshell, that's a summary of it. I'm talking about what's plausible and reasonable. As it turns out, there are some interesting passages in the Book of Acts that bring to mind the idea of plausibility and reasonableness. Can I share them with the jury now?

Defense:

Let's hear it.

Doubt:

The Book of Acts, as I've testified to earlier, is the Acts of the Apostles after the death of Jesus. It describes what they did in the days, weeks, months, years, and even decades following the Crucifixion. By the way, I'm using the term apostle here instead of disciple. Before Jesus' death, his followers, specifically the Twelve, were known as his disciples. After his death, I'm referring to them, and others, as his apostles. The word *disciple* means student and can also mean follower. The word *apostle* means messenger or someone who is sent out to spread teachings.

Once the apostles were filled with the Holy Spirit, they were able to perform miracles, including healing the sick and raising the dead. I'm not going to mention those miracles, as they are similar in type with the miracles Jesus performed. Instead, I'm going to mention passages where things were done that bring up those ideas of plausibility and reasonableness.

In the beginning of the fifth chapter of Acts, we're told there was a married couple named Ananias and Sapphira. This couple sold some property and the husband, Ananias, brought a portion of that money and gave it to the apostles, saying it was all the money from the sale of the property. Peter, who was there at the time, had special knowledge and knew that it wasn't all the money from the sale. So he admonished Ananias and asked him why he lied. When Ananias heard everything Peter said to him, he immediately fell to the ground and died. Some people hanging around saw what had happened and carried his body away. After about three hours, Sapphira came out to see what was going on. Peter asked her how much she and her husband sold the property for. When she gave the same price as her husband, Peter knew it was a lie. He admonished her for putting the Lord to the test, and she immediately fell down and died right where her husband had died. The same people who witnessed Ananias' death were there when this happened, and they carried Sapphira's body away and buried her next to her husband. [Acts 5:1-10]

According to this passage, the penalty for lying to Peter was death. The apostle, who was arguably Jesus' favorite, exacted a death penalty on two people who lied. And yet, Jesus preached forgiveness, love, mercy, and grace. How is it that the apostle who was supposed to know the teachings of Jesus the best would cut down a married couple for lying? The questions that come up are: Could this event plausibly have happened, and is it reasonable that Peter would have done this?

Just a few verses later in the same chapter [Acts 5], we read that Peter and the apostles were arrested and put in a public prison. But in the middle of the night, an angel of the Lord appeared and opened the prison doors so they could escape. The angel told them to go to the Temple and tell everyone who would gather there the message of Jesus. The apostles were obedient to the angel and, at daybreak, they went to the Temple and taught the Way of Jesus to people who gathered there. While not impossible, is it reasonable, using our twenty-first century logic, to believe an angel unlocked the prison doors? This question is not asked from a theological stance, asking if the power of God could perform this miracle; that's a theological discussion for another trial. I'm asking if, using our adult reasoning, an angel could unlock prison doors and if it is more plausible or implausible?

Another jailbreak is found in chapter 16. Paul and his companion Silas find themselves in jail. They were brought there after exposing a fortune-telling scam that caused a disturbance. The gathering crowd demanded that they be punished, so they were flogged and thrown in prison. While in prison, Paul and Silas were praying and singing hymns to God, and the other prisoners were listening to them. Suddenly, there was a massive earthquake so violent that the foundations of the prison were shaken. Immediately, all the doors of the prison opened and all the chains that were fastened to the prisoners broke loose. The jailer woke and when he saw what happened – all the prisoners free – he decided to kill himself. But Paul intervened and convinced him to convert and become a Christian.

Here again, asking the question from a logical place of understanding: Is it plausible and is it reasonable that this event took place the way it is written? This is again asked from a critical and historical perspective, not from a devotional standpoint with an apologetic appeal. Theological discussions can be held later, after this trial, regarding the power of God, the favor of Paul, and the miracles that are recorded in the Bible, and the New Testament in particular. The question here is asked from a place of knowledge and understanding of our minds where they are today. Is this incident, from a historical stance, more likely or less likely to have happened?

Going back to acts that seem counter to the teachings of Jesus, we can look at the thirteenth chapter of Acts. Here, Paul and others were preaching in what was probably an outdoor market in Cyprus. There, they confronted a magician who opposed their preaching the word of God. Paul, filled with the Holy Spirit, calls him the son of the devil and the enemy of righteousness. He then tells him the hand of the Lord is against him and he will not see for a while. As soon as he finished saying that, the man went blind.

Here, Paul uses the power of the Holy Spirit and the hand of the Lord to make someone who opposed him become blind. The teachings of Jesus never included the insistence that anyone had to accept what he was proclaiming, Sure, Jesus didn't shy away from explaining what would happen if people didn't change their way, repent, and accept him. But he never forced himself on others, and he certainly never punished anyone who didn't accept his message. Yet in this passage, Paul blinds a person who opposed his teachings – and he uses the power of the Holy Spirit and the hand of the Lord to do it. Does this sound like something Jesus would do? And is it something that, using critical thinking, is historically reliable?

One chapter before this, we learn how God strikes down the powerful. chapter 12 has another story of Peter being released from prison by an angel. This time, it was the night before Peter was to appear before Herod. Herod had a reputation as a ruthless ruler who had had enough of the trouble-making Jews now calling themselves Christians. As in the other prison stories, in the middle of the night, an angel of the Lord appeared to Peter while he was in his cell. A great light shone, and the angel tapped Peter on the side to wake him up. Peter woke up and the chains that were attached to his wrists fell off. The angel told Peter to get dressed and follow him out of the prison. Peter followed and he found himself safely outside of the city. Peter found refuge in a house, and then fled out of the area. In the morning, Herod ordered his men to look for him, and after not being able to, Herod ordered the prison guards to be killed. Herod was angry at the people of that area, but they gathered anyway to hear him give a public address from a platform. And at verse 23 it reads: "And immediately, because he had not given the glory to God, an angel of the Lord struck him down, and he was eaten by worms and died." [Acts 12:23]

Here, it's not an apostle striking down someone who doesn't accept the message of Jesus, it's the Lord Himself. Well, to be more specific, it's an angel of the Lord. It sure seems that the events documented in the Book of Acts run counter to the teachings of Jesus. Surely, if he had wanted to, Jesus could have had Herod struck down when he was still alive; and he could have had Pontius Pilate killed when he stood on trial in front of him. Instead, Jesus recognized that these leaders weren't interested in his message and so he accepted his fate – his fate according to the prophets. Once again, we are asked to consider if this event in Acts is consistent with the love, mercy, grace, and forgiveness that Jesus taught his disciples. And is an event like this – a man struck down and eaten by worms as he was delivering an address to a public gathering – more plausible or more implausible as being a historical event?

Finally, a story that sounds like it came from the old *Star Trek* TV show – a story of teleportation. In the eighth chapter of Acts [Acts 8:26-40], we're told Philip was preaching in Gaza when he came upon a eunuch who was reading the prophet Isaiah. In ancient times, a eunuch was a man who was castrated so he could devote himself to a cause other than thinking about women or sex. The Spirit of God told Philip to talk to the eunuch, so Philip obliges. A discussion ensues and Philip tells the eunuch the good news about Jesus. The eunuch asks Philip to baptize him in a small body of water that they happen to be

168

walking past. Philip baptizes the eunuch in that body of water, and when they come up out of the water, the Spirit of the Lord snatches Philip away to a city about thirty miles away, the city of Azotus. We're told that Philip then proclaims the good news to everyone there.

Philip was transported by the Spirit of the Lord more than thirty miles where he found himself walking along – passing through as it's written in the passage – the region. Again, this is not a theological issue to be debated here; instead what's being asked of us is to consider the story and ask ourselves if teleportation is more than an idea on a TV show about outer space. While it's possible for the Spirit of God to accomplish anything, what's being asked here is if, based on what we know about the molecules of the body and how they are all interconnected, a body can be dematerialized in one location and then teleported where it's rematerialized in another location.

As you can see, these stories offer ample opportunity for me to show up in the lives of those who read them. Often, I find I'm not welcomed in their lives, but I find myself there anyway. One question that must be asked is this: If you find any of these stories implausible or unreasonable, then what other passages are suspect? And when that happens, a whole can of worms gets opened. That's not to suggest, again, that these stories didn't happen; I believe what is being asked of the jury is to consider whether my existence is justified based on the facts presented in this trial. I can only ask the members of the jury to consider what I just shared and come to their own conclusions.

Defense:

I couldn't have said it any better myself, *Doubt*. But in a courtroom trial, I'm the one who addresses the jury, not you.

169

Your job is to testify. I'm sure the Judge was getting ready to tell you the same thing.

The Court:

You took the words right out of my mouth, Counselor.

Defense:

What do you say we move on to other issues, *Doubt*, other problematic passages, as you call them?

Doubt:

I wouldn't say they're passages as much as questions. And the first one is one that seems easy to answer: How many gods do Christians believe in? The answer is obvious, right? The answer is one – everyone knows that!

But has it always been just one god, and is that clearly stated in the books of the Bible?

To answer this, I need to go back into the Old Testament for just a minute. In the Book of Isaiah, in the forty-fifth chapter, God says: "There is no other God besides me, a righteous God and a savior; there is no one besides me." That should settle any uncertainty about the question, shouldn't it? It's spelled out right there – there is no other god besides God, there is no one besides God. That passage should put this issue to bed. It should, until you dig a little deeper into the books of the Old Testament.

The first book of the Old Testament, the Book of Genesis, has the creation stories. If we look at the first chapter, we read this at verse 26: "Then God said, 'Let us make humankind in our image, and according to our likeness....'" If there is only one God, who was God talking to when he said *us* and *our*? If there is no one besides God, who was God talking to and who was

God referring to when God said, "Let *us* make humankind in *our* image, and according to *our* likeness?"

To muddy the waters even more, the Book of Psalms has some interesting passages; one of them is Psalm 110. It starts off with this: "The Lord says to my Lord, 'Sit at my right hand until I make your enemies your footstool.'" Based on how this Psalm begins, is there more than one Lord? Whose Lord is speaking to whose Lord?

And one more from the Old Testament before moving to the New Testament. It's a passage that – well, it's a passage I think everyone has at least heard of. It's found in the Ten Commandments. And it doesn't matter which book of the Bible you look at that has the Ten Commandments, because it's in both lists of the Ten Commandments. It's the first commandment: "You shall have no other gods before me." Some versions say: "You shall have no other gods besides me." Another passage in the Book of Exodus, chapter 24, quotes God as saying: "For you shall worship no other god, because the Lord, whose name is Jealous, is a jealous God."

If there is only one God (that is, there is no one besides the one God), as written in Isaiah, why would the first commandment say, "You shall have no other gods before me?" If there were no other gods, why would this commandment be necessary? This first commandment suggests that God is acknowledging there are more gods than just God, and the people are not to acknowledge them. Notice God didn't say there were no other gods but God; instead, God said you shall have no other gods besides God. This is given further credence later in the Book of Exodus when God says no other gods shall be worshipped. The reason for this admonition from God is that God is a jealous God. If there were no other gods, what would there be for God to be jealous of? If a wife is flirtatious around other men, it would be understandable for her husband to be jealous. But if it was somehow possible for the husband to be the only living human male on earth, there would be nothing for him to be jealous of, right? And yet, God says God is a jealous God and no other gods shall be worshipped other than God.

Adding to these passages is one from the New Testament, from Paul's first letter to the Corinthians. In chapter 8 of that letter, Paul writes: "Indeed, even though there may be so-called gods in heaven or on earth – as in fact there are many gods and many lords – yet for us there is one God, the Father, from whom are all things and for whom we exist, and one Lord, Jesus Christ, through whom are all things and through whom we exist."

This passage brings up the question: Did Paul believe there was more than one god? He says in this passage, "as in fact there are many gods and many lords." After making this claim, Paul says that there is only one God *for us*. And that God is God the Father whose son is Jesus Christ. One could conclude, and many have, that Paul was acknowledging that there was more than one god, but Christians and the Jews before them had the one true God. Because, if he didn't believe it, why would Paul make a point to write it?

These passages have me showing up faster than just about anything in some theological discussions. They also bring me out in seminaries and other institutions of religious study. And it doesn't stop there with regards to God being the only God.

Defense:

How so, *Doubt?*

Doubt:

I think to begin, we need to agree that Christianity is a monotheistic religion. That is, Christianity is a religion that has one god and only one god. That god is the God of Abraham, a belief that claims God revealed himself to Abraham. The other two Abrahamic religions are Judaism and Islam. But this trial has the Christian Church insisting I don't belong and in fact, I don't deserve to live. So I'll stick with Christianity.

Remember, Christianity's roots are Judaism. It's based on the traditions and beliefs found in the books of the Old Testament. Jesus was a Jew and taught from the Torah. His disciples were Jews and the people he preached to were, for the most part, Jewish. So Christianity affirms what the Jewish people wrote and have believed since the writing of the books of the Old Testament: There is only one God.

Christianity also proclaims that Jesus and God are one. Jesus is God, and God is God, but there is still only one God. This was a later understanding of Jesus that developed shortly after his death. We'll come back to this later. The point I want to bring up now is there are numerous times throughout the Gospels where we read Jesus prayed. And when he prayed, he prayed to his Father. The question is: If Jesus prayed to his Father, is there one God or two Gods? If God the Father is God, and Jesus is God – God the Son – who was Jesus praying to when we read in the Gospels that Jesus prayed to his Father? Was he praying to himself?

Added to that conflict is the doctrine of the Trinity. I want to save most of my testimony on this for later, but for the purpose of this question – is there one God or more than one God – I think it needs to be brought up now. The doctrine of the Holy Trinity says there is only one God; however, this God is manifested in three Gods: God the Father, God the Son, and God the Holy Spirit. Each one of these is separately a God – yet there is only one God. Jesus was fully human, and he is also God. The Spirit is a unique entity and is also God. And the Father is God, and is *the* God.

If someone without any knowledge of the Christian religion and the doctrine of the Trinity read this logic, they would say there isn't one God, there are three Gods – it says so right there in the doctrine. But that's not the case in the Christian faith. The Christian faith says the Trinity is a mystery, that it is what can't be explained. And that doesn't matter because there is only one God.

As I said, I would like to talk about the doctrine of the Trinity at length later in this trial, but for now, I think it's important to look at this belief in one God and everything I just testified to and compare what's in the Bible to the belief in one God. But please also consider this: I am not saying there is more than one God, nor am I saying anyone is foolish to believe so. I'm asking, based on what's written about the God in the Bible and the monotheistic belief of Christians, for people to think about the problems in the sacred books that describe God. It's because of this conflict that I'm noticeable in the life of some Christians, and non-Christians as well.

And this brings me to what I'd like to get into about the traditions that developed after the death of Christ.

The Court:

I think this is a good time for lunch. There's no reason to start a new topic only to have to stop the flow of the testimony in order to get lunch in.

Any objections, Counselor?

Defense:

No objections at all, Judge!

The Court:

Great. Members of the jury, you're excused until we reconvene after lunch; get some fresh air, stretch your legs, and enjoy a good, nutritious lunch.

Chapter 9:
Early Afternoon Testimony, Day 2

*Jesus Becomes God * Who Did Jesus Say He Was? * Who Did the Disciples Think Jesus Was? * Jesus' Divinity Through the First Century * Jesus Born a Human According to Paul * Early Christian Beliefs About Jesus * Early Christian Theologies*

The Court:

Welcome back, everyone. Ladies and Gentlemen of the jury, I trust you're both well rested and well nourished.

Counselor, are you ready to continue with your witness?

Defense:

Yes, Your Honor. I'm ready.

The Court:

All right, let's get started.

Defense:

Thank you, Your Honor.

Doubt, before we took our lunch break you said you were ready to begin discussing the Christian traditions that developed after the death of Jesus. Where do you want to begin?

Doubt:

Since we finished the morning by talking about God, why not start this afternoon's testimony by continuing to talk about God? We talked about the problems in passages in the Bible that confound the monotheistic belief in the Christian God. I think it's important to understand the process that took place in order for Jesus to become God.

Defense:

What do you mean by process? Didn't people just believe that Jesus was God?

Doubt:

That's the way most people think it happened. But there was a process to Jesus becoming God. Let me explain.

I'm going to go backwards from the end of the fourth century to Jesus' ministry, and then move forward more slowly and deliberately from there. I've mentioned the Holy Trinity, the doctrine that says God, Jesus, and the Spirit are all equal in power and authority, and are all, in fact, God. Even though they are three separate beings, they are united as being just one God. In this doctrine, Jesus and God are both separate and are the same – they are both the one God. What I've found is most people don't realize that the Trinity wasn't officially accepted by the Church until the end of the fourth century. It was generally accepted before then but wasn't an official belief of the Church until the end of the fourth century.

Earlier in the fourth century, the Roman emperor Constantine called a council of bishops together to discuss the nature of Jesus and to determine in what regard was Jesus God. Before that council, there were a lot of debates and disagreements on who Jesus was in relationship to God the Father. These debates and disagreements arose from the increased distribution of the books of the New Testament as well as the traditions that were being spread by word of mouth. And as we know, the books of the New Testament were written to describe and explain Jesus' ministry and who he was.

Now, moving forward. It's important to begin with the question: Who did Jesus say he was? It would be great to get an answer to who Jesus thought he was, but that's impossible because we don't have Jesus' thoughts; all we have are his words as they are recorded in the Gospels.

In the earliest Gospel, Mark's Gospel, Jesus refers to himself as the Son of man who will sit to rule a new Kingdom of God. Jesus taught that very soon there would be a judgment of both those who were alive and those who were dead. The dead would be resurrected to stand for their judgment; that is, those who were dead would be physically raised to be judged by God. When this cosmic judgment came, the risen dead would be judged the same as those who were alive. Those who were righteous – both those who were alive and those who had been risen – would be rewarded with eternal life in the new Kingdom of God. However, those who were evil – both those who were alive and those who had been risen – would be shown their evil ways and then punished. And their punishment would be eternal death.

Jesus refers to himself as the Son of man in all three synoptic Gospels, although all three Gospels also call him the Son of God. In fact, Mark's Gospel opens by saying Jesus is the Son of God. But the question here isn't what the writers of the

Gospels called Jesus; the question is, what did Jesus call himself? If we get an answer to that question, we can infer how Jesus saw himself.

177

As I said earlier, Jesus referred to himself as the Son of man in Mark's Gospel. He also referred to himself as the Messiah who would rule over God's new kingdom after the judgment. Jesus told his disciples that each one of them would rule one of the twelve tribes of Israel after

> *Jesus preached that the Kingdom of God would be on earth, that he would be the Messiah over it, and it would be filled with those who were righteous in the way they lived their lives.*

he is seated as the Messiah. It needs to be emphasized that what Jesus was preaching was an eternal kingdom on earth. Jesus preached that the Kingdom of God would be on earth, that he would be the Messiah over it, and it would be filled with those who were righteous in the way they lived their lives. These people would have eternal life on earth.

Matthew's and Luke's Gospels have more accounts of Jesus being called the Son of God, and in these Gospels, Jesus has no objections with it. However, Jesus still refers to himself as the Son of man, as well as the coming Messiah. I should point out that the word *Messiah* means, "the anointed one." This comes from the ancient Jewish ritual of anointing a ruler, or consecrating a ruler, with special oils. It also has the meaning, "ordained by God" or "chosen by God." So when he referred to himself as the Messiah, Jesus was saying he was going to be the anointed one, or the one chosen by God to rule over the new Kingdom of God after the judgment.

I said the writers of the synoptic Gospels called Jesus the Son of God, but Jesus never called himself that. That changes when we get to John's Gospel. You might recall from my earlier testimony that in John's Gospel, Jesus uses the "I AM" title. Remember that God told Moses to tell people when they ask what God's name is, the answer is that God is "I AM." And remember that the emphasis of John's Gospel is on Jesus' divinity – to show that Jesus is God.

There is one more thing that's important to understand regarding John's Gospel. Most biblical scholars agree that there are sayings and actions recorded in the synoptic Gospels that most likely didn't happen; recall the findings of the Jesus Seminar. These scholars, as well as many theologians, believe John's Gospel is a literary book where the writers did their best to depict the nature of Jesus and demonstrate his oneness with God. The prologue in John's Gospel spells it out from the beginning:

"In the beginning was the Word, and the Word was with God, and the Word was God. He was in the beginning with God. All things came into being through him, and without him not one thing came into being. What has come into being in him was life, and the life was the light of all people. The light shines in the darkness, and the darkness did not overcome it."
[John 1:1-5]

The writer of the first five verses of John's Gospel put it out there in the beginning: Jesus is the Word, and the Word is God. It was written in a style unlike the synoptic Gospels and includes words and deeds of Jesus not mentioned in the previous three Gospels. Knowing that most critical New Testament scholars do not believe it is an accurate historical book, it is worth pointing out that this is the only Gospel where Jesus says he and the Father are one. In John's Gospel, Jesus says he is God.

There are reasons scholars and experts don't believe Jesus ever said he was God. John's Gospel is one of those reasons. The reasoning goes like this: The earliest Christian writings are from Paul, and Paul never makes any reference to Jesus and God being the same. Jesus is called the Son of God by Paul numerous times, but the title "Son of God" is used many times in the Old Testament. It's used in Genesis and in the Book of Psalms, to name just two books; David was called the Son of

179

God. So this title was not synonymous with actually being God. Moreover, Jesus never calls himself God or equates himself with God in the synoptic Gospels.

Scholars believe if Jesus had said he was God, it would have been mentioned earlier than the writing of John's Gospel. John's Gospel was written at least sixty years after the death of Jesus; surely if he had called himself God, it would have been known

> *John's Gospel is not accepted by the majority of critical scholars as being historically accurate.*

about– and talked about–earlier than the time John's Gospel was written. Paul almost certainly would have included it in one of his letters and it's unlikely the writers of the synoptic Gospels would not have heard it. And if they did hear it, it's even more unlikely that they would omit it from their Gospels. For these reasons, and more, John's Gospel is not accepted by the majority of critical scholars as being historically accurate.

Okay, I don't want this to become a bashing of John's Gospel. From a devotional standpoint, it's considered a wonderfully scripted work that describes the love and godliness of Jesus. I know I've said it before, but I feel I need to repeat it after what I just said about John's Gospel. I am not here to look at the Bible through a devotional or confessional lens. I truly honor anyone and everyone who believes in both Jesus and the words in the Bible. And personally, I believe the Bible is the most beautiful book that has ever been written. I am not here to change beliefs or convert anyone to anything. My purpose is to simply nudge the critical faculty to consider things from a historical perspective and with a critical eye. What anyone does with the information they uncover is personal and up to them; and I am okay if they consider it or discard it.

Now I think I can move on to who the disciples thought Jesus was. Consistent throughout all four Gospels is the theme that the disciples saw Jesus as their teacher who was to become the

180

new Messiah. The disciples scattered when he was arrested; their instinct was to flee, not stay with Jesus. So it stands to reason that before Jesus' death, they didn't see him as God. All that changed after his death with the Resurrection. After the Resurrection, they gained courage that they never reportedly had and went out and spread the good news of Jesus. But before his death, his disciples saw Jesus as their teacher and the new Messiah.

To make my point, I am going to refer to Mark's Gospel. Throughout Mark's Gospel, the disciples are seen as not understanding who Jesus is. They're confused, and they don't understand some of his parables. Even when Jesus tells them they will each rule one of the twelve tribes, they still don't grasp what Jesus is telling them. Finally, in the eighth chapter, halfway through the Gospel, it appears the disciples finally understand who Jesus is. In it, we read that Jesus asks his disciples who people say he is. His disciples tell him some people say he is John the Baptist, others say he is Elijah, and others say he is a prophet. Jesus then asks them: "Who do you say that I am?" Peter answers him, "You are the Messiah." To which Jesus sternly orders them not to tell anyone about him.

It seems like they finally understand. They seem to understand until a few verses later when Jesus tells the disciples that he, the Son of man, will suffer, be rejected, then arrested and killed, and three days later he will rise again. Peter apparently can't believe what he is hearing – he doesn't understand. So we're told that Peter takes Jesus aside and begins to rebuke him. Jesus responds with a well-known rebuke of his own. He looks at the disciples and says: "Get behind me, Satan! For you are setting your mind not on divine things but on human things." Just when it looks like the disciples understand.

Even though they never seem to fully grasp it in Mark's Gospel until after Jesus' death, what we can say is his disciples saw

Jesus as their teacher and the new Messiah. This is different from the way those living in the area of Galilee saw Jesus. The Gospels tell stories of the people, the Jews, thinking Jesus was a crazy guy healing the sick. Some thought he was possessed by the devil, others saw him as an apocalyptic preacher going from town to town, and some saw him as a troublemaker. What none of the Gospels say is that the people saw Jesus as God. While it's not

> *One of the reasons the Jews wouldn't have seen Jesus as God is because there was only one God. The idea that the God they worshipped could be a man would have been completely foreign to them.*

stated in any of the writings in the New Testament, one of the reasons the Jews wouldn't have seen him as God is because there was only one God. The idea that the God they worshipped could be a man would have been completely foreign to them. Sure, God could send angels, but there was no way God – the one and only God who lived in the heavens – would be a human.

Just to quickly recap, while Jesus was alive preaching his message: The people in the towns and villages he visited saw him as an itinerant preacher who healed the sick (possibly because he was either crazy or possessed by the devil), and who could stir the pot and cause trouble. Jesus' disciples saw him as the new Messiah. And Jesus called himself the Son of man or Son of God. But nowhere in any of the synoptic Gospels does Jesus refer to himself as being God, or as having equal power with God.

One question that can't be answered is: Did Jesus know he was God?

Defense:

So how then does Jesus become what we know him to be today – God? What was the process you mentioned?

Doubt:

All right. I remember when you and I were talking about what I was going to testify to and you told me about the legal term, *hearsay.* You told me I can't testify to what someone else said, even their research, unless they were here to testify after me. I can only testify to what I know, the information I remember from what I've learned, right?

Defense:

That's right, *Doubt.* Please keep your testimony to only what you know based on your own studies.

Doubt:

Okay. But let me start by saying that what I'm going to tell you now is based on significant work done at the end of the twentieth century by scholars and theologians who were well respected by their peers.

When looking at the history of the divinity of Jesus, it appears that his divinity gets pushed backwards in time as the writing of the New Testament moves forward. In other words, if there was a timeline of when people believed Jesus was divine, that moment would keep getting moved backward in time as the books of the New Testament were written. This will make more sense when I explain it.

Paul has provided the earliest writings of the New Testament that scholars have. In some of his letters, as well as the Book of Acts, Paul says Jesus became the Son of God when he was raised from the dead; that is, he was exalted to the level of Son of God at the Resurrection. He says this specifically in the Letter to the Romans and in the Book of Acts. In fact, in chapter 13 in the Book of Acts, Paul says God's promise to his ancestors was fulfilled by raising Jesus, as it is written in the second Psalm: "You are my son; today I have begotten you."

In the theological world, this is called *adoptionism*; it means Jesus was adopted by God. In this case, God adopted Jesus at the Resurrection – as it is written in the second Psalm: "You are my son; *today* I have begotten you."

Also, in the Book of Acts, in chapter 5, we read that Peter and the apostles were being questioned by the high priest. In response to his question, Peter answers: "The God of our ancestors raised up Jesus, whom you had killed by hanging him on a tree. God exalted him at his right hand as Leader and Savior that he might give repentance to Israel and forgiveness of sins." Here again is an example of adoptionism, where God exalted Jesus when he raised him from death. In this passage, like the previous one, Jesus' divinity as the Son of God happens at the Resurrection.

Remember, Paul was writing mainly in the sixth decade, starting around 50 C.E. Based on his understanding of Jesus, we can infer that at that time the accepted belief and understanding of Jesus was that Jesus was adopted by God at the Resurrection to be his Son. Then, about twenty years later, the first Gospel was written – Mark's Gospel.

In Mark's Gospel, Jesus' divinity is pushed backwards in time from Jesus' death and resurrection to his baptism, which was the beginning of his ministry. The first chapter of Mark has John the Baptist baptizing Jesus. As John is baptizing Jesus, the passage reads:

> "And just as he was coming out of the water, he saw the heavens torn apart and the Spirit descending like a dove on him. And a voice came from Heaven, "You are my beloved Son, with you I am well pleased."

So here, Jesus is exalted to the Son of God at his baptism. Mark's Gospel was written around year 70 of the Common Era. So in the year 70 C.E., Jesus' divinity is pushed back from the Resurrection to his baptism. As the decades went on, it appears the understanding of Jesus went from him becoming the Son of God at the Resurrection to him becoming the Son of God at his baptism.

Another passage that confirms this is found in the Book of Acts, in chapter 10. Here, Peter is speaking, and he is telling people that the message of Jesus spread throughout Judea after his baptism – how, at that time, God anointed Jesus with the Holy Spirit and with power. It was after his baptism that "Jesus went about doing good and healing all who were oppressed by the devil, for God was with him." This passage, along with the previous one I mentioned from Mark's Gospel, is an example of adoptionism, where God adopted Jesus at his baptism and then anointed him with the power of the Holy Spirit. Again, we see that instead of Jesus being exalted at the Resurrection, God exalts him at his baptism. So as far as Peter knew, Jesus' divinity was confirmed at his baptism. It was at his baptism, according to his most prominent disciple, that Jesus was exalted to become the Son of God.

The next Gospel written was Matthew's Gospel, written at least a decade after Mark's Gospel, in the early ninth decade of the Common Era. Matthew's Gospel pushes Jesus' divinity back to his birth. Matthew's is the first of the two Gospels that have the birth narrative of Jesus in it. In Matthew's Gospel, we read that Jesus is born to fulfill a prophecy where he will be called, "Emmanuel," which means, "God is with us." So Jesus, the newborn son, is Emmanuel; so now we know God is with us.

With Matthew's Gospel being written near the end of the first century, around 80 or 85 C.E., we can infer that the understanding of Jesus at that time was that Jesus was exalted by God at his birth. It was no longer the understanding that Jesus was exalted at the Resurrection, and it was no longer the understanding that Jesus was exalted at his baptism; the understanding at the time of the writing of Matthew's Gospel was that Jesus was the Son of God for his entire life. This is very different than the tradition that he became the Son of God – that he was adopted by God – at the Resurrection, as Paul understood it. And it was different than the tradition that Jesus became the Son of God, that he was adopted by God at his baptism, as is written in Mark's Gospel and understood by Peter in the Book of Acts. By the time Matthew's Gospel was written, the tradition was that Jesus was the Son of God his entire life. So his divinity is pushed back even further.

Luke's Gospel was written in the same decade as Matthew's, perhaps 85 to 90 C.E. In Luke's Gospel, Jesus is not only the Son of God at his birth, Jesus becomes the Son of God at his *conception* – Jesus was the Son of God in Mary's womb. We're told an angel of the Lord, the angel Gabriel, visited Mary and told her she would conceive in her womb "The Son of the Most High." A few verses later, when Mary meets with her relative, Elizabeth, she recites her "Song of Praise" where she rejoices in the privilege of giving birth to the promised Messiah.

In Luke's Gospel, not only is the birth of Jesus significant, but the conception seems to be when Jesus is exalted to the Son of God. This tradition isn't that much different from Matthew's, but it should be noted that instead of Jesus being exalted at the Resurrection as understood by Paul, and instead of Jesus being exalted at his baptism, and instead of Jesus being exalted at his birth, he is now exalted at his conception.

So it was no longer the understanding that Jesus became the son of God through adoption at the Resurrection, as was the tradition thirty-some years earlier; and it was no longer the understanding that Jesus became the Son of God through adoption at his baptism fifteen to twenty years earlier; and it was no longer the understanding that Jesus became the Son of God through his birth five years earlier. Now, the understanding was that Jesus became the Son of God the moment he was conceived.

Finally, we get to John's Gospel, written sometime toward the end of the first century, probably ten years or so after Luke's Gospel – around 95 to 100 C.E. I've already testified to the Prologue of John, the poetic introduction to John's Gospel. In it, we read that Jesus is the Word, and the Word is with God, and the Word is God. The rest of the Gospel includes numerous accounts of Jesus using the "I AM" title. He also says, in chapter 14: "Whoever has seen me has seen the Father. How can you say, 'Show us the Father'? Do you not believe that I am in the Father and the Father is in me?" And in chapter 10, Jesus says: "The Father and I are one."

For the writers of John's Gospel, Jesus was never exalted to become the Son of God. He didn't become the Son of God at the Resurrection, he didn't become the Son of God at his baptism, he didn't become the Son of God at his birth, and he didn't become the Son of God at his conception. For the writers of John's Gospel, Jesus was always the Son of God. According to John's Gospel, Jesus was God's Son from the very beginning of time; there was never a time that Jesus wasn't God's Son. In fact, John's Gospel doesn't delineate it that way; Jesus isn't just the Son of God; Jesus and God are the same: Jesus was the Word, and the Word was God.

> *For the writers of John's Gospel, Jesus was always the Son of God. Jesus isn't just the Son of God; Jesus and God are the same: Jesus was the Word, and the Word was God.*

From the beginning of Jesus' ministry to the end of the first century, a time spanning about seventy years, Jesus went from being an itinerant apocalyptic preacher to being God himself. That is a remarkable transformation to take place, in any religion, in that short a period of time. If the apostles were going about from town to town preaching that Jesus became the Son of God by being adopted by God at the Resurrection or at his baptism, how did Jesus become God just a few decades later?

That's a question that takes a bit of a tangent – again.

Defense:

Judge, is that okay?

The Court:

If *Doubt* can stay on track, I'll allow it.

Defense:

All right, *Doubt*, let's begin with a brief tangent.

Doubt:

A brief tangent, but first a little background from the earliest writer, Paul. Because Paul was the first to write about Jesus, his works are the best source we have from the New Testament of hearing what the understanding of Jesus was shortly after his death. Remember, experts in the field say Paul's conversion was one to six years after the Crucifixion; that is, within one to six years after the death of Jesus, Paul began his ministry. So, splitting the difference, we can say that about three years after the death of Jesus, Paul began spreading the good news of Jesus. Compared to the gap of four to seven decades for the Gospels to be written, three years is right on the heels of the death of Jesus. So we can assume Paul's writings reflected the understanding of who Jesus was shortly after his death.

In some of his letters, Paul gives us clues as to who Jesus was – who he was understood to be in the time shortly after his death. In Paul's Letter to the Romans, he opens by writing:

"Paul a servant of Jesus Christ, called to be an apostle, set apart for the Gospel of God, which he promised beforehand through his prophets in the holy scriptures, the Gospel concerning his Son, who was descended from David according to the flesh and was declared to be the Son of God with power according to the spirit of holiness by resurrection from the dead, Jesus Christ our Lord…" [Romans 1:1-4]

Yes, that's one heck of a run-on sentence, I know! And it goes on for a couple more lines, but the part that's important for this part of my testimony is here. And I hope you noticed where I leaned into the passage – where I emphasized what I want to talk more about. Paul says Jesus was born *according to the flesh*. He then goes on to say that he was declared to be the Son of God at the Resurrection. According to Paul, Jesus was born a human and was then adopted by God to be the Son of God at the Resurrection. Nowhere in the letter does Paul even suggest that Jesus was born a divine being. Instead, Paul says Jesus was born of the flesh and then became the Son of God when he was adopted by God at the Resurrection.

Also, in the Letter to the Romans, in the fourth chapter, Paul says we are the children of God because, *like Jesus*, we receive the spirit of adoption. Once again, I'm emphasizing the important point in what Paul is saying. Paul is in essence saying, in the same way Jesus received the spirit of adoption, that we, too, receive the spirit of adoption to become the children of God. This reaffirms what Paul said at the outset of this letter, in the first chapter: Jesus was adopted by God at the Resurrection. This is an adoptionism understanding of Jesus, one that was probably the understanding of Jesus from the time of his death until at least the time Paul wrote this letter, which is believed to be around year 57 of the Common Era.

Another letter to consider from Paul is his Letter to the Galatians. While there is no consensus among scholars as to

189

the exact date Paul wrote it, scholars do agree it was one of the earliest, if not the first, letter he wrote. Most biblical historians believe this letter was written around the year 50 of the Common Era. In this letter, in the fourth chapter, Paul writes: "But when the fullness of time had come, God sent his Son, born under the law, in order to redeem those who were under the law, so that we might receive adoption as children."

Here again, Paul is talking about being adopted by God to be his children. He also uses an interesting term that has had scholars debating it for decades. Paul says Jesus was "born under the law." Some scholars believe this indicates Paul was explaining that Jesus was born like any other Jewish child – a normal, natural human birth, Others argue that this term means something completely different. My testimony isn't to try to convince the members of the jury which biblical experts they should believe regarding this passage. Instead, I wanted to point out that once again, Paul is at least referencing the normalcy of Jesus' birth and the idea of adoption.

If we say Jesus died around the year 30 of the Common Era, we can then say that Paul's Letter to the Galatians was written about twenty years after Jesus' death, and Paul's Letter to the Romans was written about twenty-seven years after his death.

Knowing this, we can infer that the common understanding of Jesus for at least twenty-seven years following his death was he was born a human and at the Resurrection, he was adopted by God to be the Son of God.

We can infer that the common understanding of Jesus for at least twenty-seven years following his death was he was born a human and at the Resurrection, he was adopted by God to be the Son of God.

I wanted to use this early understanding of Jesus as the foundation of what I want to get to now.

190

Defense:

Which is?

Doubt:

The early Christians, and what they believed. First, I want to talk about their understanding of Jesus, then their theology based on that understanding, and finally, the early Christian sects that developed between the end of the first century and the early part of the fourth century. The books of the New Testament inspired a diverse set of beliefs about Jesus and God, leading to the development of early Christian sects.

I'd like to start by giving a bulleted list of sorts. This is a list that contains the various beliefs about Jesus in the time from the end of the first century, when the last books of the New Testament were finished, until the Council of Nicaea, which convened in the year 325 C.E. I think this list will help demonstrate that diversity of beliefs I just mentioned. Here it is:

- Jesus was born human and became divine at either his baptism, resurrection, or his ascension.
- Jesus had a human body, but a divine mind; the seat of his emotions was his lower soul.
- Jesus was subordinate to God, as was the Holy Spirit; Jesus was created as the Son of God and therefore not God by nature, but he was different than all other creatures because he was the direct creation of God.
- Jesus' physical body was an illusion; because he was a pure spirit, he could not have a physical body and did not actually die.
- Jesus was a man in flesh, and Christ was a separate entity who entered Jesus' body in the form of a dove at his baptism, empowered him to perform miracles, but abandoned him on the cross upon his death.

191

- Jesus was the human son of Mary who came to emphasize the Mosaic, or biblical, Law.
- Christ was *of* two natures – human and divine, but not *in* two natures; his natures were blended in such a way that Christ had a human nature, but it was unlike the rest of humanity.
- Jesus was a savior sent by the True God to liberate souls trapped in the material world.
- Jesus was a false messiah who perverted the teachings taught to him by John the Baptist.
- Jesus was divine and created the Holy Spirit.
- Jesus' mission was to overthrow the fickle, cruel, and despotic God of the Old Testament and replace him with the supreme God of love whom Jesus came to reveal.
- Jesus Christ was the incarnation of the Divine Word and identified with the Holy Ghost.
- God the Father suffered on the cross – not God the Son in the form of Jesus.
- Jesus had two natures, but only one will; therefore, he was not fully divine.
- Jesus had two persons: the divine Logos – God's Word, and the human Jesus.
- Christ came down from Heaven to emancipate humans from the body and from the world.
- Christ was the son of a female God from a complex celestial system.

Now, is that a list, or what?

How many did I lose halfway through this list? You're not alone, trust me. With all these different understandings of who Jesus was, with all these beliefs about Jesus, is it any wonder different sects developed rather quickly in the early Christian Church?

A more relevant question might be this: Do any of these beliefs about Jesus sound even remotely similar to the Jesus portrayed in Mark's Gospel – an itinerant apocalyptic preacher proclaiming a cosmic judgment where he would be the Messiah in the coming Kingdom of God?

Not to add more confusion to the mix, but I think it's important to also see how many different beliefs about God came from these understandings of Jesus, to see the different theologies that developed because of the them. Here is a list of beliefs:

- The soul perished with the body, and both would be revived on Judgment Day.
- God had human form; taken literally from the text in Genesis, God created mankind in His own image.
- The church must be a church of saints, not sinners; anyone who sought martyrdom was a saint.
- The essence of the Trinity could be perceived by the carnal senses, and God takes different forms to reveal Himself to the senses.
- A state of perfection – freedom from the world and passion – can only be attained by prayer; it can't come from the church or any of its sacraments.
- There are two worlds: the material world and the spiritual world. The material world was created by a fallen, or evil, spirit; the God of the Hebrew Bible was this fallen/evil spirit. Jesus was the Savior, sent by the True God into the material world to liberate the souls trapped there.
- God the Father and Son were equal, but the Holy Spirit was created by the Son and was a servant of the Father and Son.
- The God of the Old Testament and the God of the New Testament were two different gods; the Old Testament God was evil, and the New Testament God was love.

Therefore, Jews were not good people, and Christianity should be based solely on love.

- God is one person appearing and working in the three different modes of the Father, Son, and Holy Spirit.
- Christians are too worldly; they need to return to primitive Christian simplicity, prophecy, celibacy, and self-discipline.
- Christ did not exist in the flesh. The serpent in the Garden of Eden was a hero, and the God that forbade Adam and Eve to eat from the tree of knowledge was the enemy. Christ imitated Moses' serpent's power, so worshiping the serpent was preferred over Christ.
- Even though God's grace assisted every good work, human will was sufficient to live a sinless life.
- Different gods ruled over different attributes of humans; Christ stood next to the supreme female principle, Sophia, and that he was the son of Sophia.

Another interesting list, wouldn't you agree? And somehow, the Christianity that we have today either came through some of these theologies or survived them – depending on how you look at it. A question similar to the one I asked regarding the previous list is this: Do any of these beliefs sound anything like the Jewish beliefs that were the basis for Christianity – believing in and worshipping one God and keeping the law and the traditions as told in the ancient books of the Old Testament?

I think it's interesting that before Jesus, the Jewish people had a relatively simple belief system; sure, there were some weird laws, and a bunch of them at that. But, all in all, it was a fairly easy to understand religion. Along comes Jesus with his rather simple belief system and teachings: repent and prepare for the judgment of God, forgive others, don't repay a bad deed with a bad deed – simple teachings like that. But shortly after he died, within just a few years, things began to get complicated.

And things didn't get any simpler or easier to understand in the decades, and centuries that followed.

With that said, I'd like to go into the different sects that developed as a result of these beliefs about Jesus and about God.

Defense:

Will this be another bulleted list, *Doubt*?

Doubt:

I don't think listing these would do them justice. I'd like to talk about each one to show the similarities and dissimilarities to what we know as Christianity today.

The Court:

Counselor, if I may interrupt?

Do you plan on completing your examination of *Doubt* today?

Defense:

Yes, Judge. My plan is to complete my examination and offer the jury my closing arguments tomorrow.

The Court:

Can I assume that there is still more material you intend to get through before we recess for the day?

Defense:

Yes, Your Honor. There is more material after *Doubt* testifies about the different Christian sects that developed. And I would really like to get all of *Doubt's* testimony about it to the jury so tomorrow is just my closing arguments.

The Court:

In that case, seeing that it looks like we're in for a longer afternoon than yesterday, let's take two breaks this afternoon. That way, the members of the jury will stay fresh and I'll be able to stay fresh, as well.

Defense:

No objections, Your Honor.

The Court:

Good, we'll take a short recess so all of us can come back with fresh minds and with relaxed bodies.

Chapter 10:
Midafternoon Testimony, Day 2

*The Different Sects in the Early Christian Church * Orthodox Views in the Early Church * The Holy Trinity * The Arian Controversy and the Council of Nicaea * The Johannine Comma*

The Court:

Good afternoon, once again, ladies and gentlemen of the jury. Now that you've had a chance to stretch your legs and quench your thirst or enjoy a snack, it's time to get back to the reason you're here: to listen to testimony and evaluate the credibility of the witnesses.

Counselor, if you're ready to proceed, let's continue with *Doubt*'s testimony.

Defense:

Yes, Your Honor, we're all set.

Doubt, you finished your testimony on the different beliefs that were developed about Jesus in the years, then decades, after his

197

death. Also, you gave testimony on how those beliefs and understandings of Jesus changed people's understanding of God – how it shaped their theology. Was that testimony the basis for what you want to talk about this afternoon?

Doubt:

Yes. Now that the members of the jury have an idea of the different beliefs that developed about Jesus, as well as beliefs about God, it's time to explain how these beliefs became different sects in the early Christian Church. I have a list to read to you, and to make it easy, I put it in alphabetical order. Sit tight, it's quite a list.

I mentioned the term *adoptionism* earlier this afternoon. This was the belief that Jesus was born fully human to his parents, Joseph and Mary. Depending on the sect, he became divine at either his baptism, his resurrection, or his ascension. This belief was declared a heresy by the end of the second century and was formally rejected by the Council of Nicaea in 325 C.E.

Apollinarism was the belief that Jesus had a human body and a lower soul, which was thought of as the seat of the emotions. This was named after a bishop, Apollinaris of Laodicea. He believed that Jesus had a divine mind and that the souls of men were propagated by other souls, as well as their bodies. This belief was declared a heresy in 381 C.E. at the First Council of Constantinople.

The *Arabici* sect was a small sect of Christians who believed that the soul perished when the body died, and that both would be revived on the judgment day. The founder of Arabici is unknown, but it's associated with third-century Christians from Arabia. They were called Arabici by St. Augustine because they flourished in Arabia. However, they only lasted about four decades after persuasive mediation by an early Christian theologian named Origen at a council in 250 C.E.,

198

when they were reconciled back into the main body of the Church.

Arianism is named for Arius, a priest in Alexandria, Egypt. Arius became known for his *subordinationism* teachings, which stated the Son, Jesus, and the Holy Spirit were subordinate to God the Father. This belief held that the Son of God was not eternal, but was created by the Father as an instrument for creating the world. He was not God by nature, but was different from everyone else because he was the one direct creation of God. It has been called the most challenging heresy in the history of the Church and believed to be the biggest reason the emperor Constantine convened the First Council of Nicaea.

Audianism is a sect named after its founder, Audius, who lived in Syria. Audians were around in the fourth century in Syria and eastern Europe. They took the text in Genesis literally – that God created mankind in his own image – so they believed God had human form. It was condemned a heresy at the First Council of Nicaea.

Docetism is named for the Greek phrase, "to seem" or "to appear." It's a broad teaching that Jesus' physical body was just an illusion. That is to say, Jesus only seemed to have a physical body. In reality, he was a pure spirit, so he couldn't physically die. This was first mentioned by a bishop in Antioch around the year 200, who used the apocryphal Gospel of Peter as the basis for this belief. Some Docetism beliefs claimed that Jesus was a man in the flesh, but Christ was a separate entity who entered Jesus' body in the form of a dove at his baptism (which empowered him to perform miracles) and abandoned him when he died on the cross. It was explicitly rejected at the First Council of Nicaea.

Named after a Christian bishop in North Africa, Donatus Magnus, *Donatism* was a faction of the Church that flourished

199

in that part of the region during the fourth and fifth centuries. Donatists were considered to be rigorists who believed the Church must be a church of saints, not sinners. They also said that sacraments administered by any clergy who avoided persecution by the Romans were invalid, and that martyrdom was the supreme Christian virtue; anyone who actively sought martyrdom was a saint. Donatism was condemned a heresy by Pope Miltiades in 313 C.E.

The *Ebionites*, known as "the poor ones," were a sect of Jewish Christians who flourished in the early centuries of Christianity, especially east of the Jordan River. They believed Jesus was the human son of Mary and that he emphasized the Mosaic law. They practiced severe self-disciplines and abstention and were devout vegetarians. They rejected Paul's epistles, and used only one gospel, the Gospel of the Ebionites – a shortened and modified version of the Matthew's Gospel. They were declared heretical in the middle of the second century.

The *Euchites* originated in Mesopotamia and spread throughout Asia Minor in the middle of the fourth century. Their name comes from the Greek, meaning, "one who prays." Their beliefs included that the essence of the Trinity could be perceived by the senses, saying God takes different forms in order to reveal himself. They believed the perfection of God is attained solely through prayer, not by the Church or any of its sacraments. Euchites taught that once a person experienced the essence of God, they were free from moral obligations and religious discipline. They were condemned a heresy by Bishop Flavian of Antioch around the year 376.

Eutychianism was a doctrine that became widespread throughout many parts of the Middle East and India from the end of the fourth century through the middle of the fifth century and is attributed to the ideas of Eutyches of Constantinople, a presbyter and abbot of a monastery outside the walls of Constantinople. Followers of Eutychianism believed the human nature of Jesus was overcome by the divine, and that Christ had a human nature but it was unlike the rest of humanity. Eutyches maintained that separate divine and human natures had united and blended in such a manner that although Jesus was being with the Father, he was not being with man. Eutyches was denounced as a heretic at the Council of Chalcedon in 451 C.E., which adopted a statement of faith known as the Chalcedonian Creed that directly addressed and condemned the doctrines of Eutyches.

In the ancient Greek world, the word *gnosis* meant secret knowledge (over the millennia, it has come to simply mean knowledge). *Gnosticism* became a popular generalized theme of several distinct Christian sects around the turn of the first century. *Gnostics* considered the material world to be a prison created by a fallen or evil spirit who they said was the God of the material world. Secret knowledge, or gnosis, was believed to liberate a person's soul to return to the true God. Jesus was the Savior, a spirit sent from the true God into the material world to liberate the souls trapped there. Gnostics believed in a dualistic universe of light and dark, spirit and matter, and good and evil. Gnosticism was condemned as a heresy by the end of the second century.

Founded in the mid fourth century, the *Macedonians* accepted the divinity of Jesus Christ, but they denied that the Holy Spirit was one with God. Instead, they believed the Holy Spirit was a creation of the Son (Jesus) and a servant of the Father and Son. They were condemned at the First Council of Constantinople in 381 C.E.

In 144 C.E., the Church in Rome expelled the son of a bishop, Marcion of Sinope; he then set up his own religious organization, later called *Marcionism*. Their core belief was that there was a huge difference between the God of the Old Testament and the God of the New Testament: The God of the Old Testament was evil, and the God of the New

Testament was love. Marcionists were vehemently anti-Jewish in their beliefs and accepted only the Luke's Gospel. Marcion later wrote his own gospel, which was his own version of Luke. Marcion argued that Christianity should be solely based on Christian love; he went as far to say that Jesus' mission was to overthrow the evil and cruel God of the Old Testament, and replace him with the supreme God of love whom Jesus came to reveal. Biblical scholars and theologians credit his writings for having a profound effect on the development of Christianity and the canon. However, Marcionism was declared a heresy at the Council of Nicaea in 325 C.E.

Modalism is attributed to Sabellius, a Roman priest and theologian, who around 215 C.E., shared his belief that God is one person, in direct contrast to the Trinity. This belief held that God was one person appearing and working in the three different modes of the Father, the Son, and the Holy Spirit, hence the name, modalism. It also claimed that God the Father suffered on the cross, not Jesus the Son. Modalism was condemned as a heresy by the bishop of Rome around the year 262.

Known as the "doctrine of one will," *Monothelitism* was the view that Jesus Christ had two natures but only one will. During the fifth century, debates were rampant over the nature of Jesus after the First Council of Nicaea declared heretical the notion that Jesus was not fully divine. This belief was strongly held by many in the Church until the middle of the seventh century when the doctrine was rejected completely by Pope John IV.

Around 156 C.E., a priest from Asia Minor named Montanus launched a ministry of prophecy criticizing Christians as being too worldly. This became known as *Montanism*. He preached a return to primitive Christian simplicity, prophecy, celibacy, and self-discipline. The sect spoke in tongues, and many theologians believe they were the foundation from where Pentecostals formed their beliefs. Montanus' followers revered him as the Paraclete, the advocate, that Christ had promised. His sect spread across the Roman empire. It became such a threat to the orthodoxy and growth of the Church, that in the sixth century, Justinian the Great ordered the sect's extinction.

Nestorius was the Archbishop of Constantinople in the early fifth century. He believed Jesus had two persons: the divine Logos and the human Jesus. He also believed that Mary was not the Mother of God, but instead, she was the "Bringer forth of Christ." This became known as *Nestorianism*. This belief became so strongly held by many that it created a schism in the Church, with Nestorian theology pitted against a more literal view of the New Testament. It was denounced as heretical in the mid fifth century at the Council of Ephesus.

One of the earliest Christian Gnostic sects, the *Ophites*, believed that the serpent who tempted Adam and Eve was a hero, and that the God who forbid Adam and Eve to eat from the tree of knowledge was the enemy. They further believed that Christ did not exist in the flesh, and that he imitated the power of Moses' serpent. They exalted the serpent and preferred it to Christ, and even included the serpents in their Eucharist celebrations. Their beliefs were denounced as heretical in the early third century.

Paulicians were a Christian sect that flourished throughout Armenia from the middle of the seventh through the middle of the ninth century. They were adoptionists and gnostics, accepting a combination of dualistic and Christian doctrines. Although they accepted the four Gospels, they rejected the Old Testament. They further believed that Christ came down from Heaven to liberate humans from the body and from the world. The founder of the sect believed he was called to restore the pure Christianity of Paul and adopted the name Silvanus, one of Paul's disciples. Twenty-seven years after founding his first congregation, he was stoned to death for heresy in 687 C.E. Ironically, the court official who ordered the execution converted to the same beliefs and adopted the name Titus. He was found guilty of heresy and was burned to death as his punishment. Paulician communities were still found in different villages up until the end of the nineteenth century.

Named after Pelagius, a fourth-century British monk and theologian who advocated free will, *Pelagianism* was a belief that original sin did not influence human nature and that mortal will was still capable of choosing good or evil without divine aid. Pelagius taught that although God's grace assisted all good works, human will was all you needed to live a sinless life. Pelagianism was condemned as heresy in 431 C.E. at the Council of Ephesus.

Valentinianism was a Christian gnostic movement founded by Valentinus who was a candidate for bishop of Rome in the first half of the second century. Its theology was extremely complicated, and adherents developed a complex celestial system where different Gods ruled over different attributes of humans. Part of that belief was that Christ was equal with and the son of a supreme female principle. Valentinianism was declared a heresy almost immediately after it started.

And, umm—

Defense:

Doubt, please tell us that's all you got!

The Court:

I second that!

Doubt:

I know, quite a list, right?

I wanted to share these divisions of the early Church because I think it's important to see just how many factions of Christianity developed in such a short period of time after

Jesus' death. You would think that Jesus' message was simple: He preached love and forgiveness and mercy and hospitality. But shortly after his death his message and his identity became convoluted through the acts of men – they were all men, of course – who believed that each had the correct beliefs about Jesus. The word for having the correct belief is *orthodox* or *orthodoxy*. Each of the sects that came out of the Jesus tradition of the second half of the first century believed they had the orthodox understanding of Jesus and his message. Had any of these beliefs gained enough traction to attract more converts, if any of these sects became more prominent and popular, we all might be practicing a completely different type of Christianity than what is found in churches today.

And that's why I thought it was important to share this list. I know it is a long one, but it allows the members of the jury to consider some things on their own about the early development of the Christian Church. If nothing else, it shows you how different people can believe their understanding of something is the right one – that is, the orthodox view. It's also worth noting that the people or institutions that declared each one of them heresies believed their beliefs and teachings were the orthodox ones.

Defense:

So the people who believed their views were orthodox – they believed they had the authority to declare the others heresies?

Doubt:

Exactly! So imagine for a moment if one of the factions on the list I shared had enough power and followers to declare what are now the

Imagine if one of the factions had enough power and followers to declare what are now the current beliefs of the Christian Church to be heresies. What would our worship services look like if the Trinity had been declared a heresy?

205

current beliefs of the Christian Church to be heresies. What would our worship services look like if the Trinity was declared a heresy back in the second and third centuries? If that had happened, the Council of Nicaea probably would have been debating something completely different when they convened in the early part of the fourth century.

Defense:

I'm not sure if the members of the jury would find that interesting or find that possibility scary. I mean, the idea of the Trinity as a heresy is something that certainly doesn't sit well with me. At least it's based on a solid biblical foundation. So we can move on to the next topic.

Doubt:

Actually, it's not.

Defense:

What's not?

Doubt:

The Trinity isn't based on a solid biblical foundation.

Defense:

It has to be! Otherwise we wouldn't say, "In the name of the Father, the Son, and the Holy Spirit," all the time in church. What are you saying, *Doubt?*

Doubt:

Okay, I know I'm not going to increase my chances of winning a popularity contest with the jury, but I promised to tell the truth. And as I've said so many times throughout this trial, what I'm going to share is taught in every seminary in the world, and has been for hundreds of years. It's taught in theological schools and other institutions of higher learning –

so this is nothing new to any member of the clergy or any graduate of these schools.

So here goes.

The Holy Trinity is a concept that came from an early Christian author and apologist from the second century named Tertullian. In this context, the term *apologist* means someone who defends the teachings and beliefs of the Church. Along with many other early Church apologists, Tertullian was trying to figure out the nature of Jesus and his relationship with God and the Spirit. While not a lot is known about how he came up with it, Tertullian coined the term *trinity* to describe the unique oneness of God, Jesus, and the Spirit.

The issue being discussed and argued at that time was the unmoving belief that there was only one God. Early Christians who claimed to have the orthodox view insisted that this new faith would not be a polytheistic religion but would remain a monotheistic religion. Since it was based on the God of the Old Testament, they didn't want to take away that understanding. But if God was God, and Jesus was God, don't you have two gods? And if the Spirit is also God, then don't you have three gods?

Early Church fathers insisted that Jesus was both fully human and fully God. So they had Jesus as God, and his Father as God. Which meant there were two Gods. But they were insistent that this was a monotheistic religion, so there could only be one God. And no matter how they tried to explain it, they kept coming away with the problem of more than one God. If you want to see some examples of this, feel free to go back and check out some of the early Christian beliefs I shared just a little while ago.

Tertullian had what I guess was a brainstorm of an idea: There was only one God, the one true God. And yet, Jesus was God as was the Spirit. All three were separate, yet they were only

207

one God. And he called this the Trinity. When questioned, "How can there be only one God if God is God, and Jesus is God, and the Spirit is God; don't you have three Gods?" His answer was: "It's a mystery." Problem solved. And if you think you understand it, you don't understand it at all.

Defense:

Well then, I'm not going to respond that I understand it!

So that was it, that's how we got all three are equal and there is only one God.

Doubt:

Not quite.

Defense:

What do you mean?

Doubt:

Tertullian started the concept, but he wasn't the one to finish it. That would come later at the Council of Nicaea. You see, Tertullian believed God the Father was superior to God the Son and God the Holy Spirit. He also believed that only God was preexistent from before the beginning of time; Jesus was created by God the Father, as was the Holy Spirit. I should point out that Tertullian was very interested in the sect I included in my list, Montanism, which remained popular into the sixth century.

Although early Church fathers accepted Tertullian's concept of the Trinity, they were divided as to what extent was Jesus God. This led to what became known as the Arian Controversy. If you recall from the list of early Christian sects I shared, Arius believed that Jesus, although God, is subordinate to God the Father. He also believed that Jesus was not eternal from before time, but was created by God the Father as an instrument for

208

creating the world. Although Arius accepted Tertullian's concept of the Trinity, he did not believe Jesus was equal with God. This belief did not sit well with some of the early Church fathers who believed the orthodox understanding was that Jesus was always existent with God the Father – just like with God the Father, there was never a time before which Jesus did not exist. And so this created a controversy in the Church that became known as the Arian Controversy.

Arius was a priest and his bishop disagreed with his view. Arius' bishop held to a different belief that had developed: that the divine nature of Jesus was identical to that of God the Father, and the Father and the Son are of the same substance. Furthermore, they have coexisted since the beginning of time. Thus, the Arian Controversy.

Defense:

You said this controversy was resolved at the Council of Nicaea. What was the Council of Nicaea?

Doubt:

I have a feeling this might be a slightly different answer than a lot of people believe. The Council of Nicaea was a group of bishops from throughout the Roman Empire that was convened per the order of Constantine, who was the emperor then. The council convened in 325 C.E. in the city of Nicaea in what is now modern-day Turkey. Their main purpose was to iron out the Arian Controversy – that is, Jesus' nature in relationship to God the Father.

As some background, Constantine converted to Christianity around the year 312. He is believed to have converted sometime after a vision he had before going into a battle. Constantine soon realized how much better it would be to have a united empire instead of one split by factions arguing who had the orthodox belief. The division caused by the Arian

Controversy became such an issue that Constantine wanted it decided once and for all. Historians say Constantine didn't have an opinion on it; he didn't care which way the decision went, all he wanted was for it to be decided.

Arius and his bishop debated in front of the Council, and after the debate, Arius lost. The Council voted overwhelmingly in favor of adopting the official belief that Jesus, the Son, is equal to and has always been with God, the Father. Jesus the Son and God the Father were identical in divine nature and of one substance. For his part in the controversy, Arius was booted out of the Church.

Many people mistakenly believe that the Trinity was voted on at the Council of Nicaea. It needs to be said that by the time the Council met, the Trinity was generally accepted. In fact, Arius himself believed in the concept of the Trinity. Other theological issues were voted on by the Council, but its main purpose was to decide the Arian Controversy. And out of the agreement that came from it, also came the origins of the Nicene Creed that is read in many churches today.

Defense:

So there we have it: The official Church doctrine of the Holy Trinity was decided in 325 at the Council of Nicaea.

Doubt:

Nope.

Defense:

Seriously, *Doubt?*

Doubt:

Seriously.

But can I go back and address the Nicene Creed really quick?

Defense:

Sure, go ahead.

Doubt:

There are a lot of people who believe the Nicene Creed, as it's read in churches today, came from this Council of Nicaea. In fact, the creed that came out of this Council of Nicaea was more like a rough draft of the one we have now. The Nicene Creed that is recited today is a refined version that came out of a different council, the First Council of Constantinople in the year 381.

The original Nicene Creed had an ending that might shock those who've never heard it. It goes like this: "But those who say: 'There was a time when he was not;' and He was not before he was made;' and 'He was made out of nothing;' or 'He is of another substance' or 'essence,' or 'The Son of God is created,' or 'unchangeable,' or 'alterable' – they are condemned by the holy and apostolic Church." Can anyone imagine reciting this ending in church?

You see, the members of the Council wanted to not only send a strong message about what would be tolerated, they also wanted to address some of the heretical beliefs, and sects, that had cropped up. If you go back and check out the list I shared, you'll see how this old, original ending did just that.

Okay, that's it regarding the Nicene Creed – for now.

Defense:

So now we can get back to the Trinity becoming the official Church doctrine.

Doubt:

The council of bishops that met agreed that this belief in the Holy Trinity was the orthodox understanding. However, it didn't become the official Church doctrine – that is, the Doctrine of the Holy Trinity – until the later part of the fourth century. But questions about it continued from then until our present time.

Defense:

Why is that? If you know.

Doubt:

I can't say I know definitively, but I do have an opinion.

Defense:

What is your opinion on it?

Doubt:

My opinion is that the Holy Trinity wasn't part of the official doctrine because it is not based on any of the books of the Bible, either the Old Testament or the New Testament. While there are insinuations to it that nibble at the edges of this belief, Jesus himself never taught it, nor did any of the apostles, including Paul. While the books of the New Testament mention Jesus as the Son of God, and they mention God the Father, as well as the Spirit, nowhere are the three of them said to be one with each other. This concept came to a second-century Christian author and apologist who called it a mystery. It was after Tertullian's belief became known to the early Church fathers that they began searching the books of the New Testament to uphold Tertullian's claim.

I believe because the Trinity is a man-made construct, it leaves itself open for questions and scrutiny by Christians and non-Christians alike. The Holy Trinity was not Jesus' teaching, it wasn't Paul's teaching, and it wasn't the teaching of any book in the New Testament – when they were written.

Defense:

What do you mean by, "when they were written?"

Doubt:

Do you remember when I just said the concept of the Holy Trinity does not appear in any of the books of the Bible?

Defense:

Yes.

Doubt:

Well, that was a truth that wasn't quite truthful. In a way—

Defense:

In what way, *Doubt?*

Doubt:

I know I swore to tell the truth, the whole truth, and nothing but the truth; but I believe after hearing what I have to say, the Judge will agree I still told the truth based on a technicality. A New Testament passage supporting the Holy Trinity showed up for the first time in the Greek manuscripts in the thirteenth century – 900 years after the Council of Nicaea. This will take a little bit of explaining.

Remember that the entire New Testament was first written in Greek; every book was written as a Greek manuscript. Scribes then copied these manuscripts so they could be distributed to other churches. So our best references are the Greek manuscripts that have survived to today. Recall also that I testified to how scribes changed the manuscripts – either accidentally or purposely. In a letter in the New Testament known as the First Epistle of John, or "First John," a passage appeared that supported the Holy Trinity.

213

I talked about this in my earlier testimony, this passage is called the Johannine Comma. From the oldest known Greek manuscript of First John, through the time of the Council of Nicaea, up to the beginning of the thirteenth century, this passage was not in any of them. None of the ancient Greek manuscripts predating the thirteenth century had this passage that supported the Holy Trinity. It wasn't until the thirteenth century that this passage first appeared in the Greek manuscripts. It's important to understand here that there were no Staples or Office Depots where you could go with a manuscript and get copies made. If you wanted a copy made, you hired a scribe who copied the manuscript page by page, line by line, word for word, letter for letter. And as I said, scribes were known to change manuscripts – again, either accidentally or purposely.

Somewhere in the early thirteenth century, a scribe added the passage to First John. It's believed by scholars that this scribe probably heard a tradition that was circulating, possibly from church sermons, that referenced First John as being the book that supported the Doctrine of the Holy Trinity. After it appeared in the first manuscript it gradually gained prevalence in other manuscripts. In the sixteenth century, a Dutch Christian scholar brought the comma to the attention of the Church. Since that time, most Bibles have a footnote to the passage or have it in brackets with a margin note. Other copies of the New Testament leave it out altogether and others include it with no notes or citations.

Defense:

So the technicality you described is the fact that this passage, the Johannine Comma, wasn't in the Epistle of First John when it was first written, is that right?

Doubt:

That's correct. And instead of helping to confirm the Doctrine of the Holy Trinity as having biblical authority, it only made suspicions worse. To summarize this part of my testimony, the Doctrine of the Holy Trinity came about from a belief of a second century Christian author and apologist who called it a mystery if asked to explain it. The Church made it an official belief after a council of bishops determined the true nature of Jesus. Nine hundred years later, a passage supporting the Trinity appeared in a letter written by an unknown person. For about three hundred years, copies of this passage were included in this letter and in Bibles that were distributed throughout the world. Even after the Church was made aware of the addition, the passage has remained in most Bibles that have been published since the discovery of it.

And people wonder why I show up when I do.

Defense:

That's what this trial is about, *Doubt*. And I think the picture you're painting for the jury is getting clearer and clearer.

Doubt:

That's all I can ask of them.

And if I can say this without sounding like a broken record, this history of the Trinity is taught in every seminary and in every theological school in the world.

Defense:

I don't think it's a broken record, *Doubt*. I see it as a good reminder for the jury.

Now that we've concluded this part of your testimony, maybe this is good time to take a short break – if that's agreeable to the Judge.

The Court:

Counselor, do you intend to conclude your examination of *Doubt* when we return from this break?

Defense:

Yes, Your Honor, that is our plan. We'd like to finish our examination of *Doubt* and conclude with him addressing the jury with one last statement. Then, tomorrow morning, I'll be delivering my closing statement.

The Court:

Okay, I agree that a short break is in order; after all, we're going to go on through this afternoon until *Doubt* is finished with his testimony. Let's take that break now, and when we come back in session, *Doubt* will conclude his testimony.

Chapter 11:
Late-Afternoon Testimony, Day 2

*The Trinity: One God or Three Gods? * Substitutionary Atonement * Christian Victimization * Christian Persecution Before Constantine * The Early Creeds * Closed Canon of Scripture * Agnosticism in the Church * God's Nature * Transactional Theology * The Problem of Suffering * Theodicy*

The Court:

Ok. We're in the homestretch now. I want to take a moment to thank the members of the jury for your attention and your patience during this trial so far. You've all been attentive and engaged in the testimony, and I want to let you know that it hasn't gone unnoticed. I'm sure both sides appreciate it as much as I do.

Now, with that said – Counselor, are you ready to proceed?

Defense:

Yes, Your Honor, we're ready, and I know my client is looking forward to sharing with the jury his last bit of testimony.

The Court:

And I'm sure they can't wait to hear it. Just remind him to stay on track. It's getting late.

Defense:

I will, Your Honor.

Doubt, did you hear the Judge's comment?

Doubt:

I am sitting right next to him – how could I miss it? I mean, yes, I understand. I'll keep my answers on topic and my tangents brief.

Defense:

We all appreciate that.

Doubt, before the break you finished testifying about the Trinity. Let's move on to other Church doctrines. What are the other doctrines that people find troubling, other Church beliefs that cause you to show up in people's lives?

Doubt:

I want to mention just one more, but before I do, I want to go back to the Trinity for just a minute. When people discuss the Trinity, what I most often hear them say is that there is one God, and he appears and works in three different ways – as the Father, the Son, and the Holy Spirit. In my experience, this seems to be the most logical answer to the question: How can there be only one God if there is God the Father, God the Son, and God the Holy Spirit? It makes sense and at least offers an explanation other than what Tertullian gave – that it's a mystery.

There's a problem with that belief, however. And it's this: The notion that God is one God and he appears and works in three different ways was ruled a heresy in the middle of the third century. Early Church fathers insisted that God didn't operate in three different modes, a belief called modalism; God was God, the one and only God. However, they also insisted on acknowledging three separate entities – that God the Father was a separate entity from God the Son and God the Holy Spirit; that God the Son was separate from God the Father and God the Holy Spirit; and that God the Holy Spirit was separate from God the Father and God the Son.

Since the time it was made an official Church doctrine, people have been debating how there can be only one God if the three "versions" of God are each God themselves. Don't you have three Gods? The most logical answer to that question was ruled heresy soon after it became a belief.

The other doctrine that has me showing up in people's lives, and even in churches, is the doctrine of *substitutionary atonement*, also called penal substitution atonement. This is also called a theory by some people. It's the belief that Jesus was crucified to atone for the sins of humanity. In other words, Jesus died for our sins. It's certainly something most people have heard – whether inside a church or outside.

This belief says, in part, that it was God's plan for Jesus to suffer and die, to sacrifice his son, in order to forgive the sins of the world. While it sure seems like a very noble thing to do, it has caused distress in some people who think about it being more than a theory. And when spelled out, their concerns do appear to have some merit to them.

A little background is needed for this to be fully understood. The concept of original sin is that God's perfect creation was corrupted by original sin; all humans are sinful in nature because of what happened in the Garden of Eden at the beginning of the Book of Genesis. According to that account, God created perfection – the earth, and man, and woman. But then, Adam and Eve disobeyed God, so God cursed them as a punishment. That curse was hard labor for Adam, painful childbirth for Eve, and death for both of them. The concept of original sin, or ancestral sin, is that since they sinned against God by disobeying God, all their offspring were also sinful. So every human who came through the ancestry of Adam and Eve is sinful in nature – the concept of original sin.

To save humans from their sin, their original sin, God sent Jesus into the world to ultimately bear the price for their sins. This is the view that came shortly after Jesus' death – that he died as a sacrifice for the sins of others. The thinking at the time of Jesus' death was because Jesus was blameless, he must have died for the sins of others. In this way, Jesus was like a special rescue operation: to rescue, or save, humans from their sins so they could have eternal life – a life that was put back into perfection.

Here's the problem some people have: If God sacrificed his only son, what does this say about the nature of God? Does God require a blood sacrifice in order to satiate some unknown need? There are numerous passages in the New Testament where Jesus forgives without asking anything in return, and even more passages where he instructs us to forgive without asking anything in return. Taking the Trinity into account, is God the angry Father God who demands a sacrifice, or is God the loving Son God who says our sins are forgiven? If God the Father requires someone to pay the price for our sins, namely Jesus, does God really ever forgive anyone without a payment?

Can sins really be transferred from one person to another? Remember, Jesus was said to be fully human according to the orthodox understanding of him. If sins can be transferred, what are we to make of God the Father being so angry toward Jesus, God's son, that he punished him knowing that Jesus never did anything wrong? Was Jesus' purpose on earth to appease his Father's wrath – a human blood sacrifice because of what others had done? Finally, if the Trinity is correct, that Jesus is God and was God from the beginning of time, wouldn't that mean that God sacrificed God?

I need to point out to the jury that my job isn't to take sides on this or any belief. It's not up to me to say whether this doctrine is in line with the books in the Bible or the teachings of Jesus. I bring it up here to demonstrate for the jury that the questions I asked about it are some of the problems people have with it, and that often brings me to the table as well.

Defense:

To clarify, you didn't ask all those questions about the doctrine of substitutionary atonement to question the theology surrounding it. You brought them up as examples of what people have wondered about it. Is that correct, *Doubt?*

Doubt:

Yes, precisely. Again, I'm not here to talk about the orthodoxy of theological beliefs; that's a debate for a different venue. It doesn't matter to me what someone believes. I honor all beliefs or disbeliefs. I mentioned those questions because they are a few of the problems that reside in the hearts of some people when they discuss the doctrine of substitutionary atonement. And where there are questions like these, I usually find myself in there as well.

Defense:

Ok. Let's move on.

Doubt:

Before we do, can I add one thing to what I just testified to?

Defense:

Sure, *Doubt.* What is it?

Doubt:

Going back to substitutionary atonement. I should have included this when I was talking about it, because it's another issue some people have with this belief. And that's this: Jesus is the chronic victim in it. The concept of original sin says every human is sinful, dating all the way back to Adam and Eve. With the substitutionary atonement belief, God demanded someone to pay for the sins of everyone but him. In this belief, Jesus becomes the victim of our sins. He becomes the sacrificial lamb. Jesus is the victim when he is betrayed, when he is arrested and abandoned by everyone who knew him, when he is tortured, when he is mocked, when he is humiliated, and when he is crucified. He is the ultimate victim when he is killed because of the thoughts, words, and actions of others.

But it goes even further. Jesus becomes the victim of a wrathful God who demands a human blood sacrifice; he is the victim to a God who can't forgive unless a price is paid; he is the victim to a God who picked someone who preached forgiveness and turning the other cheek instead of fighting back; and he is the victim to a God that contradicted the very lessons Jesus taught – especially the one about "an eye for an eye." Think of what this has done to people throughout the millennia. People feel guilty for being responsible for making God having to take the action that God took.

Guilt and fear are probably the two emotions that have kept people in check more than any others since time began. With substitutionary atonement, guilt is added to the sadness people feel over the torture and Crucifixion of Jesus. It's our fault that Jesus was killed;

> *Guilt and fear are probably the two emotions that have kept people in check more than any others since time began. And instead of taking responsibility for our bad deeds and shortcomings, an innocent man was sacrificed so that we might have eternal life. God is the bully, Jesus is the victim, and we get off scot-free.*

222

because we are such lousy people, Jesus was killed. Instead of us taking responsibility for our bad deeds and shortcomings, an innocent man was sacrificed so that we might have eternal life. God is the bully, Jesus is the victim, and we get off scot-free.

Getting back to Jesus as the victim. Christians were persecuted in the first couple hundred years before Constantine's conversion. Christians were victims of persecution, torture, and death. This new religion, whose central figure was a victim, was victimized by those filled with hatred toward them. The apostle Paul talked frequently in his letters about how he and the other apostles were victims of beatings, false allegations, and imprisonment.

Under the belief of substitutionary atonement, some people see this as having created a religion where Jesus and his followers are victims. Whenever there is a victim, there is at least one person or entity that is the one doing the bullying. Some might call this person or entity the victimizer. And very often, when given the opportunity, when one feels victimized, they also become a victimizer.

Think about how the Christian Church has victimized others since its inception: During the Crusades, Muslims were victimized by Christian armies; during the founding of this country, Native Americans were victimized by Christians claiming manifest destiny, and blacks were victimized by Christian slave owners; during the civil rights movement, blacks were again victimized by Christian churches; during the fight for equal rights, women were victimized by Christian employers; and today, the LGBT community has been victimized by Christian clergy and elected officials. The victim mindset becomes a vicious cycle. And often the behavior in that cycle is fueled by hatred, fear, and even guilt.

And it creates at least one more issue.

Defense:

What's that, *Doubt?*

Doubt:

Distorted history.

Defense:

How so?

Doubt:

Historians point to many sources that document the persecution, torture, and killing of Christians in the first three centuries. There is no question it happened. But it didn't happen to the extent and degree most people believe.

Like I said, there is no question that in the first three hundred years of Christianity, people in the Roman Empire who practiced Christianity were persecuted – sometimes arrested, sometimes beaten and tortured, and sometimes even killed. But what most people think they know about it is usually distorted by biases. For example, many people believe Christianity was an outlaw religion in the Roman Empire, that it was illegal for someone to practice Christianity before the reign of Constantine. Some people believe Christians regularly went into hiding in the Roman Empire, and that they routinely hid in the catacombs under the city of Rome to avoid being found. And some believe that people couldn't openly profess their faith, that they weren't allowed to openly practice Christianity.

Historians now tell us that Christianity was never declared an illegal religion in the Roman Empire. And even if it were to be declared illegal throughout the empire, enforcement of empire-wide edicts was, at best, haphazardly enforced. Different regions of the empire had their own rules and regulations, and the way they enforced them was up to local officials from each region.

When persecutions did happen, they were sporadic and not empire-wide. Most early Christians lived their entire Christian lives with no problems from the Roman government. Again, that's not to say persecutions and the horrible acts associated with them didn't happen; they did. As I said in earlier testimony, Paul wrote about his arrests and beatings. What needs to be said about them is historians believe most of Paul's arrests and beatings were because he was seen as a troublemaker, and in the Roman empire, troublemakers were punished. No law needed to be broken; if someone was a troublemaker, a local official could determine that and what the punishment would be.

The emperor Nero was the first emperor to have problems with Christians. But not for the reasons a lot of people think. In the year 64, a good portion of Rome was burning, and some people were blaming Nero for starting it. Nero needed a scapegoat, and he chose the Christians to blame for starting the fires in Rome. Historians today say he chose the Christians because, as the ancient Roman historian Tacitus wrote, "The Christians were the hatred of the human race." Nero used informants to identify Christians, then had them arrested and subjected to punishment, including torture and horrific deaths.

This was the first emperor-ordered persecution of Christians, but it was localized to the city of Rome. And the Christians were persecuted not for being Christians, they were punished for the charge of arson. Even though they didn't commit the act, Nero used them as scapegoats to get the pressure off of himself. So he had them arrested and punished.

There were other persecutions of Christians after Nero's reign, but none were empire- wide nor organized. That is, until the reign of the emperor Decius. Decius was emperor for less than three years, and they were three very bad years in the Roman Empire. The empire was starting to show cracks in its power and solidarity; there was an economic collapse and natural disasters; and there were two breakaway states and barbarian invasions, as well as assassinations and assassination attempts on officials. Needless to say, it was not a fun time to be the emperor.

Decius decided he and the entire empire needed the gods on their side in order to get the Roman Empire back on track to its old self again. So he implemented a policy that said everyone in the empire had to perform an animal sacrifice to please the gods, and each person had to produce a certificate showing they did in fact perform an animal sacrifice to the gods. Decius hoped an empire-wide sacrifice to the gods would satisfy them and they would protect the empire and bring it back to its previous standing.

Based on the teachings of Jesus, Christians could not make an animal sacrifice. So Christians were not punished for being Christians; they were punished for not making the required sacrifice. Previous beliefs that Decius did this solely to persecute the Christians have changed in the academic world. Scholars have investigated it and they are almost in consensus that he did it for his own religious reasons: to please and satisfy the gods so they would take care of the empire.

The major persecution of Christians occurred in the early fourth century with the reign of the emperor Diocletian. In the year 303, Diocletian enacted an empire-wide attempt to wipe out the Christians. His edicts included: ordering church buildings to be destroyed and Christian scriptures be confiscated; ordering clergy to be arrested and thrown in jail; and ordering all Christians to perform a sacrifice. And he said clergy could only get out of jail if they performed a sacrifice to pagan deities. Anyone who disobeyed the edicts was arrested, punished, tortured, and sometimes executed. This was called

226

"The Great Persecution." It was arbitrarily enforced and where it was enforced, it wasn't enforced equally. Also, it was very rarely enforced in the western part of the empire.

This was a ten-year edict, and it continued after Diocletian was no longer emperor. During the ten years it was going on, one of the emperors converted to Christianity. His name: Constantine. And when Constantine converted in the year 312, he ordered a halt to any persecution of Christians.

I offer this brief history lesson because I believe facts matter. I know the jury is going to be asked to consider the facts of this trial, and not preconceived beliefs they entered the courtroom with. I also want them to understand that I'm not saying Christians weren't persecuted or that some of them didn't experience terrible ordeals including torture and death. They did! I would submit that too many of them did.

Defense:

With all that being said, *Doubt*, is it your testimony that there was persecution of Christians before Constantine's reign, but the degree of that persecution is less than what a lot of us thought to believe?

Doubt:

That's exactly the point of what I just shared.

Defense:

Okay. We're getting near the end of your testimony, *Doubt*. What else do you think is important for the members of the jury to hear so they can arrive at a verdict that is fair and just?

Doubt:

I think it is important for them to consider the creeds that came out of the fourth century.

Defense:

Tell the members of the jury what you want them to know about the early Christian creeds.

Doubt:

There were no less than eighteen creeds that were written in the fourth century. These were documents that came out of different councils that met to clarify a theological understanding or understandings, and each creed claimed the orthodox beliefs about God and Jesus. I want to briefly talk about just two of them. These two are arguably the best known of the fourth-century creeds: the Nicene Creed and the Apostles' Creed.

I talked about the Nicene Creed in earlier testimony, so I'm not going to go into much more detail about it. The Apostles' Creed was written about sixty-five years after the Nicene Creed and is believed to have been included in a letter from the bishop of Milan. It's called the Apostles' Creed because the writer believed the Twelve Apostles, under the inspiration of the Holy Spirit, all contributed to its contents. And because it was predated by other creeds that were already established, it does not specifically address the Trinity or the divinity of Jesus or the Holy Spirit.

For comparison, here are the two creeds in their 1970 English translations.

The Nicene Creed:

> We believe in one God, the father almighty, maker of heaven and earth, of all that is, seen and unseen. We believe in one Lord, Jesus Christ, the only Son of God, eternally begotten of the Father, God from God, Light from Light, True God from True God, begotten, not made, of one Being with the Father. Through him all things were made. For us men and for our salvation he

228

came down from heaven: by the power of the Holy Spirit he became incarnate from the Virgin Mary and was made man. For our sake he was crucified under Pontius Pilate; he suffered death and was buried. On the third day he rose again in accordance with the scriptures; he ascended into heaven and is seated at the right hand of the Father. He will come again in glory to judge the living and the dead and his kingdom will have no end. We believe in the Holy Spirit, the Lord, the giver of life, who proceeds from the Father and the Son. With the Father and the Son is worshipped and glorified. He has spoken through the prophets. We believe in one, holy catholic and apostolic Church. We acknowledge one baptism for the forgiveness of sins. We look for the resurrection of the dead and the life of the world to come. Amen.

The Apostles' Creed:

I believe in God, the Father almighty, creator of heaven and earth. I believe in Jesus Christ, his only Son, our Lord. He was conceived by the power of the Holy Spirit and born of the virgin Mary. He suffered under Pontius Pilate, was crucified, died, and was buried. He descended to the dead. On the third day he rose again. He ascended into heaven and is seated at the right hand of the Father; He will come again to judge the living and the dead. I believe in the Holy Spirit, the holy catholic Church, the communion of saints, the forgiveness of sins, the resurrection of the body, and the life everlasting. Amen.

The first thing you might notice is that the Nicene Creed is twice as long as the Apostles' Creed. Since the theology of the Trinity was worked out in the Nicene Creed, the writer of the Apostles' Creed apparently didn't find it necessary to rehash it in his creed. Another difference is how in the Nicene Creed, the beliefs are from *we*: We believe in one God... We believe in one Lord... and so on. Whereas, in the Apostles' Creed, everything is *I believe in*: I believe in God... I believe in Jesus Christ... and so on. The Nicene Creed uses the first-person plural pronoun, we; and the Apostles' Creed uses the first-person singular pronoun, I.

Remember that the Nicene Creed came from an agreement that was ironed out by a large group of bishops. In the fourth century, the only bishops were men. In the latter half of the twentieth century, Christian denominations began removing the word men in the line that begins: "For us men and for our salvation..." The newer, more

> *In the Nicene Creed, notice how patriarchal the Church was and how long it's taken for women to be seen as equals in it.*

inclusive text that is just about universal in all churches now reads: "For us and for our salvation." What's important here is to take notice how patriarchal the Church was and how long it's taken for women to be seen as equals in it.

Notice how both creeds use the term "catholic Church" – catholic with a lowercase c. Used with a lowercase "c," the word *catholic* means universal or all-inclusive; it doesn't mean the Roman Catholic Church. The Nicene Creed refers to "the catholic and apostolic Church," indicating the Church comes from the work of the apostles.

One final thing to point out: Both creeds include the Resurrection. In the Nicene Creed, it's the resurrection of the dead, and in the Apostles' Creed, it's the resurrection of the body. Recall how Jesus preached a cosmic event where both those living and those who were already dead would be judged. What's interesting is that while the Nicene Creed is vague with its reference to "the dead," the Apostles' Creed is specific that there will be a resurrection of the body.

I hope that my testimony during the past two days has given you a chance to see these creeds through a different perspective, in a new light, and with a new appreciation. And I think it's important to remind ourselves that we are using twenty-first-century logic to interpret fourth-century thinking of first-century beliefs by men who knew almost nothing about the ancient religion on which those beliefs were based. I often wonder why some theologians haven't gotten together to come up with another creed that is inclusive and welcoming, a creed based on our twenty-first-century understanding of Christianity. Maybe it's for the same reason most of our church's liturgy for its sacraments and rites hasn't changed since the thirteenth century.

Defense:

Do you know the reason, for this, *Doubt?*

Doubt:

No, I don't. I would assume it has to do with the closed canon of scripture.

Defense:

So the jury understands, what is the closed canon of scripture?

Doubt:

The canon of scripture are the books of the Bible. The canon is closed, meaning no other books can be added to it. By the end of the fifth century, every Christian church had agreed that the twenty-seven books of the New Testament were the books of the New Testament, and there would be no others. In a way, I think it's a shame. If we accept that Jesus was God, and that Paul spoke for God since he received his knowledge from visions from God and Jesus, why can't we accept what other religious people have said as being worthy of being included as

231

a sacred scripture? Why would God stop talking to us 2000 years ago?

Sure, it might sound like a rhetorical question, but there have been historical figures since the canon was closed that certainly merit discussion as to their words and their works being inspired by God. And we don't even have to go that far back in history. Think of what Gandhi did and said. Think of the impact Martin Luther King, Jr. had on the world with his words and his actions. Consider the artwork of Artemisia Gentileschi; the songs and struggles of Gladys Bentley; and why not the words from Fred Rogers, who was an ordained Presbyterian minister, as well as Dr. Seuss? Imagine if we gave their lives – their words and actions – the same reverence as we do the books in the New Testament, books that were written by men decades after the events in them took place?

Defense:

That is definitely some food for thought, *Doubt*.

And that's a good reminder for the jury that the Gospels were written between forty and seventy years after the events in them took place.

Doubt:

Exactly!

Here's an experiment to try. Think of an event in your life from forty years ago. Now, if you're not yet forty, think of an event that took place when you were in middle school. Any event, just something memorable that happened. Now, try to recall the details of that event – what happened, who was with you, the conversations with people who were there, the location. Things like that. Got it? Good.

Now, think of what it would be like if you were asked to record everything memorable that happened that entire year. Think of what that would be like. And make sure it's in chronological order – you know, week to week, then month to month – for an entire year. Not easy, is it? Now you have to translate that story into a language you never spoke.

How accurate would your testimony be if you were asked to describe in detail what had happened, in the order it happened, including places and people who were there, all while making sure you get the conversations exact? Every word that was said in those conversations needs to be exactly as they were uttered forty years ago. What would the chances be that the year-long story you told was accurate and exact in that different language?

Now you have an idea what the writers of the Gospels were up against.

Defense:

Talk about a tall order! I'm sure the members of the jury really do appreciate the difficult job that the writers of the Gospels faced. And it makes it easy to understand why you have shown up so often in the life of the Church.

Doubt:

Often, I show up when and where I'm least expected. And I think this leads to people exploring their beliefs and sometimes changing their certainty of them. Which can then lead to an agnostic view of the books in the Bible, as well as an agnostic stance on the beliefs of the Church as a whole.

Defense:

Doubt, I think it's important, as we wrap up your testimony, that the jury understands why people see themselves as agnostic. Can you give the jury your opinion as to why people are agnostic?

Doubt:

I think the answer to that is very personal to each person who says they're agnostic. I wouldn't pretend to know the "why" to that question. What I can testify to is my opinion of the environment that opens the door for agnosticism.

Defense:

And what is that?

Doubt:

I would call it God's nature.

Defense:

What do you mean by *God's nature*?

Doubt:

I mean God's mood, God's timing, God's character. It seems that when you dig into the books of the Bible, you find polar opposites of God's mood, God's timing, and God's character: God doing and saying things that go against the character most people were taught.

For instance, most people grew up being taught, and then believing, that God is a loving and just God, a God who sees and treats each person as his child, that God is our father, and people are his children. Here are some passages from the Bible that tell us how much God loves us:

- In First John, chapter 4: "Beloved, let us love one another, because love is from God; everyone who loves is born of God and knows God. Whoever does not love does not know God, for God is love."
- In Second Chronicles, chapter 6: "He said, 'O LORD, God of Israel, there is no God like you, in heaven or on earth,

keeping covenant in steadfast love with your servants who walk before you with all their heart…'"

- In Psalm 36: "How precious is your steadfast love, O God! All people may take refuge in the shadow of your wings."

- In Psalm 109: "But you, O LORD my Lord, act on my behalf for your name's sake; because your steadfast love is good, deliver me."

- In Micah, chapter 7: "Who is a God like you, pardoning iniquity and passing over the transgression of the remnant of your possession? He does not retain his anger forever, because he delights in showing clemency."

- In Paul's Letter to the Romans, chapter 5: "… and hope does not disappoint us, because God's love has been poured into our hearts through the Holy Spirit that has been given to us."

- In Jeremiah, chapter 29: "For surely I know the plans I have for you, says the LORD, plans for your welfare and not for harm, to give you a future with hope."

- In Psalm 86: "But you, O Lord, are a God merciful and gracious, slow to anger and abounding in steadfast love and faithfulness."

- In Paul's Letter to the Romans, chapter 8: "For I am convinced that neither death, nor life, nor angels, nor rulers, nor things present, nor things to come, nor powers, nor height, nor depth, nor anything else in all creation, will be able to separate us from the love of God in Christ Jesus our Lord."

- In Deuteronomy, chapter 7: "Know therefore that the LORD your God is God, the faithful God who maintains covenant loyalty with those who love him and keep his commandments, to a thousand generations…"

- In the book of the minor prophet Zephaniah, chapter 3: "The LORD, your God, is in your midst, a warrior who gives victory; he will rejoice over you with gladness, he will renew you in his love; he will exalt over you with loud singing…"

- In John's Gospel, chapter 3: "For God so loved the world that he gave his only Son, so that everyone who believes in him may not perish but may have eternal life."
- In the Book of Isaiah, chapter 54: "For the mountains may depart and the hills be removed, but my steadfast love shall not depart from you, and my covenant of peace shall not be removed, says the LORD, who has compassion on you."
- In Psalm 136: "O give thanks to the God of heaven, for his steadfast love endures forever."

That's quite a list, don't you think? And this is just a sampling of the passages in the Bible that remind us of how much we are loved by God. There are also passages about how much God loves children; in fact, in Matthew's Gospel Jesus says: "Let the little children come to me, and do not stop them; for it is such as these that the kingdom of heaven belongs." [Matthew 19:14]

God loves each one of us as a unique child, and God loves small children, too. I'm reminded of the church hymn, "Jesus Loves the Little Children." We receive reassurance from the books of the Gospel and reassurance from the hymnal of God's love for us and the children.

And here is where the issue of God's nature comes in; some might call it God's quirkiness. Because, as much as we're told in the Bible and in our hymns that God loves each one of us, especially the children, there are no less than fourteen accounts in the Bible where God kills children. Fourteen passages that describe God killing children for a variety of reasons. And these fourteen specific times do not include a horrific account in the Book of Exodus where God killed every first-born child in Egypt. The number of children killed by God can't be counted because we don't have an estimate of how many first-

236

born children there were in Egypt when this happened. If this account is true, it's possible that tens of thousands of children were killed by God.

It needs to be said that biblical scholars and historians don't give this story very much weight as being a historical event; there is no record or evidence of it anywhere outside this passage in the Book of Exodus. So here again we have a passage that exemplifies the problem of biblical literalism. But the writer of the Book of Exodus had his reason for putting it in the chapter. One can assume the writer included it to demonstrate God's character: Was it to teach a lesson, to punish someone, to persuade someone? No matter the reason, the passage shows God's willingness to kill innocent children. Were the children in Egypt guilty of anything other than being born to their parents in that part of the world?

I offer this as an example of the environment created for agnosticism because of God's nature. If God is a loving God, as stated in the passages I listed, how is killing innocent children an act of love? And if God especially loves children, why would he kill so many of them?

Defense:

These are some difficult questions, *Doubt.* I'm assuming you aren't asking them rhetorically.

Doubt:

No, I'm not. These questions tug at the hearts of a lot of people. And before they know it, there I am in their faith journeys. And, unfortunately, this is just one problem with God's fickleness. Do you want to hear more?

Defense:

If you think they're important to the members of the jury to consider.

Doubt:

I think they're very important. I mentioned the killing of children in the Bible, and there are also numerous accounts where God kills people by the thousands – even tens of thousands, and millions. Of course, there are also accounts where God kills individuals and families.

If someone was asked if they knew the number of times in the Bible God kills people, I think they would be shocked by the passages that document these killings, and the total number of people killed. There are no less than 135 passages in the Bible where God either condones, orchestrates, or does the actual killing, torturing, or mutilating of people for a variety of reasons. I'm not going to go into the details of these killings, but I would encourage the members of the jury to research for themselves the number of times in the Bible where God kills.

Not including plagues, the great flood where Noah built the ark, massacres, wiping out armies, and wiping out towns, God is responsible for allowing, condoning, orchestrating, or actually killing more than 2.1 million people – that's the number you get if you add up all the figures the writers of the books in the Bible give. If we take into account the massacres and the armies that were wiped out by God, the towns and villages destroyed, and the great flood that reportedly killed everyone but Noah's family, that number is exponentially higher.

If we go back to the list of passages I began this part of my testimony with, we'd read that God is a loving God and we are safe with him. But if we read the 135 passages that describe killings attributed to God, we see a completely different version of God. So it begs the question: What kind of God is God? Is God the loving God we find in certain passages, or is God the vengeful and wrathful God found in the 135 passages that detail his brutal power?

This is the confusion agnostics deal with, and why I am in their lives when they consider Christianity and the nature of God.

Defense:

Are there other reasons?

Doubt:

Regarding confusion and God's nature? There are plenty. But I'll only mention a few more.

The Old Testament is filled with stories of suffering. Some of them were condoned or orchestrated by God. Why would a loving God allow Job to suffer the way he did? If God is an all-loving God, why would he allow one of his children to suffer? What kind of father is that? Why would God get a large fish to swallow Jonah and have Jonah trapped in the fish's belly for three days? What kind of God does that?

In the twenty-second chapter of Genesis, we read how God tested Abraham by telling Abraham to sacrifice his son, Isaac. Abraham obeyed God and gathered wood for the fire, carried Isaac to the place where it was to be done, built an altar for the sacrifice, and then laid his son on the altar. One can only imagine what was going through Abraham's mind at this time.

Abraham drew his knife and raised it over Isaac, ready to plunge it into his son, when suddenly an angel of the Lord appeared and told Abraham not to do it. This angel complimented Abraham for his faithfulness in, and fear of, God. Assuming God saw Abraham as his child, as we are all God's children, the question begs to be asked: What kind of father does this to his son? What kind of father would put his son through this? If God is a loving God, why would God require this kind of test to demonstrate one's faith in him and fear of him?

God reportedly flooded the whole earth killing every living creature; this was done out of anger. Plagues were sent to people who were just trying to survive. Millions of people were killed by God's hand. Why? What kind of God does these things? How can God be called a loving God if God did all the things that are documented in the pages of the Bible. Who is holding God accountable?

These questions aren't mine, of course. These are questions I hear repeatedly when I'm present in the lives of people who question things and who use critical thinking to consider different passages in the Bible. They think: Is it any wonder people drop to their knees when they pray to God? And when they pray, either in private or in church, they plead for mercy? Christian prayers and biblical passages are filled with pleas for mercy. What kind of relationships come to mind when someone drops to her or his knees in the presence of the master and then begs for mercy? Does a loving God require this kind of worship and fear?

And speaking of prayer, why does God answer some prayers and allow others to go unanswered? Someone is thrilled when they get that perfect parking space at the mall they prayed for while a child, lying in a hospital bed down the street from the mall, dies from a horrible disease in spite of his parents' prayers for healing. Why? Why are some prayers answered and others unanswered? I will tell you that members of the clergy get asked this question a lot. Hopefully, their answers don't include any reference to certain people being more deserving than others.

Thankfully, very few – a tiny fraction – of clergy would say that to a grieving parent. Most answers to the questions of prayer is that God's ways are mysterious, and we simply can't understand them. I find it interesting that for a lot of people, God gets a pass regardless of whether a prayer is answered or unanswered. If a prayer is answered, people say, "God is good." You see it on social media sites all the time – when someone posts good news about their progress in a disease or illness, their friends often comment, "God is good." But when a prayer isn't answered, people say things like, "God had other plans for you," or, "God is healing her differently than what we understand." Whether God answers a prayer or not, it seems like Christians have a response. There's a response that praises God when a prayer is answered, and there's another response that doesn't hold God accountable when a prayer isn't answered – some call it an excuse. It's as if we're afraid to be angry at God. Maybe that's because of the 135 passages that describe God's anger and God's power.

Defense:

Doubt, I want to make sure the members of the jury understand something about your last answer: Your testimony is from what you've heard from people and not your opinion – is that correct?

Doubt:

I'm sorry; yes. I should have been clearer. What I'm testifying to is what I've heard over the years, the decades, and centuries I've been around. I've been invited into conversations, debates, and arguments because the testimony I just gave was an issue for someone. And, of course, there are times when I'm not invited – I just show up unannounced. That's just *my* nature.

Defense:

Understood. Thank you for clarifying this part of your testimony.

I said just a few minutes ago that we're wrapping up your testimony. Are there other reasons people of faith have questions regarding God's nature?

Doubt:

There is one that has more to do with people than with God; but it dovetails nicely with what I just testified to. There are many places in the New Testament where we read passages that tell us if we pray, God will answer our prayers. And we read in some parts, mostly in Paul's letters, that since God gave his only son as a sacrifice, we owe God something in return – to be good Christians, being grateful and being willing to do good in the name of Jesus.

I've heard this type of understanding being called *transactional theology*. Transactional theology is just what it sounds like: There's been a transaction and both parties expect something in return. I like to think of it as consumerism Christianity, where people are the consumer and God is the retailer. Sometimes, I picture God as a vending machine, with someone standing in front of it, holding a dollar bill, looking at the possible selections. The person puts the dollar into the machine, makes a selection, and the item drops to the bottom tray for the person to take.

In this scenario, the dollar represents the person's prayer. The person makes a *transaction* with God: I put in the prayer, you give me what I requested. This is all well and good until the time comes when the dollar goes in the machine, the item is selected, but nothing happens. Nothing drops to that bottom tray. The person pushes and pushes the button for the selection harder and harder, still nothing.

Since God is perfect, there can't be anything wrong with the machine; there must be something wrong with the person making the selection. Or, maybe something was wrong with the dollar bill. When prayers go unanswered, I usually enter the picture. And this is when I hear people saying to themselves things like there is something wrong with them – they don't have enough faith, or they've done something wrong that they're being punished for, or they didn't pray hard enough.

Instead of using prayer to transform their expectations, some folks I've met expect the transaction to be completed as per the contract: They did their part, so they expect God to do God's part. It's a trap that often leads to low self-esteem and feelings of despair. I guess what I'm trying to get across to the jury is that it's not always God's fault when we think about God's nature.

Defense:

That's good to know, *Doubt*. After all, people are only human. So it looks like that's it for God's nature. Unless you have anything else?

Doubt:

Just one more that I'd like to bring up: the topic of suffering.

Most people who believe in Jesus, those who say they're Christian, believe at least a couple of things about God. Theologians have called these "the Omnis of God." The prefix *omni-* comes from Latin meaning *all*. These are the beliefs that are common among all Christians, regardless of denominations: God is *Omniscient* – that is, God is all-knowing; God is *Omnipotent* – that is, God is all-powerful; and God is *Omnipresent* – that is, God is everywhere at the same time. I would submit to the jury that in addition to these beliefs, Christians also believe God is *Omnibenevolent* – that is, God is all-loving and filled with unlimited goodness. There are also beliefs that God is just and fair. I'd like to look at just two of these universal understandings of God with regard to suffering: that God is all-powerful, and that God is all-loving.

But first, I'd like to point out how the Bible deals with the issue of human suffering.

If you look at different passages, you get different answers to the question: Why does God allow suffering? Some passages say suffering is the punishment for disobeying God. Other passages say there is suffering because of evil forces in the world that oppose God. Some parts of the Bible say there is suffering because God is testing people's faith. Some writers in the Bible explain suffering as a mystery no one can ever understand, and it is blasphemous to even question it. And some writers in the Bible say chaos just happens.

Since as far back as anyone can remember, people have asked, "How can God be just and all-powerful and all-loving if there is so much suffering in the world?" We acknowledge God is all-powerful, we acknowledge God is all-loving, we acknowledge

> *How can God be just and all-powerful and all-loving if there is so much suffering in the world? For some people, these four truths can't be true at the same time.*

God is just, and we also acknowledge that there is suffering. For some people, these four truths can't be true at the same time. Their logic goes like this: If God is all-powerful, God can certainly take away suffering. If God is all-loving, God certainly does not want us to suffer. And if God is a just God, God would make sure the righteous don't suffer as much as the shitheads in the world.

I'm sorry, that last part slipped out. What I meant to say is if God is a just God, God would see to it that the people who do good suffer far less that those who are evil. So the thinking is that God can't have all of these attributes and still allow suffering.

One theodicy is to take away one of the understandings of God. If you—

Defense:

Wait, *Doubt.* Did you say *theodicy?* What's a theodicy?

244

Doubt:

Theodicy means to justify God or to defend God – an all-loving and all-powerful God – who, with all that power and love, still allows evil and suffering in the world. It's a philosophical or theological defense or justification or vindication of God in view of the existence of evil and suffering.

Defense:

Thank you for explaining that for the jury. Go ahead with your testimony.

Doubt:

Okay, where was I? That's right – one way that people resolve the issue of God's involvement in suffering, or God's inability or unwillingness to stop suffering, is to remove one of the three beliefs I mentioned that Christians have about God, the three truths of God:

1. God is all-powerful.
2. God is all-loving.
3. God is just.

Some people remove an all-powerful God from the equation, so you have an all-loving and just God who allows suffering. Some people remove an all-loving God from the equation, so you have an all-powerful and just God who allows suffering. And others remove a just God from the equation, so you have an all-powerful and all-loving God who allows suffering. Some believe this is the reason why the righteous suffer while the evil ones prosper.

One truth that can't be removed is suffering. No one denies that there is suffering in the world. And while there are explanations for why God allows bad things to happen, why God allows people to suffer, it's all but impossible to explain away natural disasters that leave thousands, sometimes hundreds of thousands, of people suffering. The fact that innocent people are left desolate after a natural disaster really bothers people who struggle with me in their lives. People who were just in the wrong place at the wrong time, people who didn't do anything to evoke God's wrath, are a real issue for people like you.

Defense:

That makes sense.

Wait – what? What do you mean a real issue for people like *me*?

Doubt:

Hey, when I put my hand in the air yesterday morning and swore to tell the truth, I swore to tell the *whole* truth.

Defense:

Yeah, but I never told you—

Doubt:

All those conversations we've had since shortly after seminary. All the research you've done since your ordination. All those times I've showed up unexpectantly, as well as those times you invited me into your life? What, you didn't think I knew all this time that you see yourself as an agnostic? And, as a Christian minister, you're having a difficult time accepting it?

Defense:

Doubt, now hold on a minute! This trial is about you, this trial isn't about me.

Doubt:

Isn't it also about the people whose lives I show up in? Shouldn't they have a say? Even if it's just one person?

Defense:

Your Honor, may I have a word with my client?

The Court:

Has your witness become a hostile witness, Counselor?

Defense:

I'm not sure what's going on, Judge; I would like a few minutes to find out. I think it's only fair for everyone concerned.

The Court:

And I think it's only fair for the members of the jury to hear what the Defense's one and only witness has to say. So I'm going to order *Doubt* to continue with his testimony.

Defense:

But Your Honor, I must object to—

The Court:

Overruled!

Doubt, continue with your testimony.

Doubt:

Thank you, Judge.

Defense:

Okay, *Doubt*. Now that you've outed me as an agnostic minister to the jury, what would you like to tell them about me? Better yet, what do you want to say about me to anyone who picks up a transcript of this trial and reads it? Wouldn't it be ironic if someone turned it into a book one day?

Doubt:

I would tell them this:

I was there when your parents were diagnosed with cancer. You didn't want me in your life then, you wanted to believe they would beat the disease. You and your brother were just teenagers and you had to deal with both your parents being diagnosed with cancer. I watched you pray for their healing. I was there when your mom got sicker and sicker; it seemed the harder you prayed, the worse she got. And I was there with you when she died. You were so young.

I was there when your dad got worse and I remember all those nights sitting with you as you prayed your heart out that you wouldn't lose him, too. When you got the phone call from the hospital on that Thanksgiving morning after your mom died – I heard the words the nurse spoke, telling you that your dad died sometime during the night. He died alone.

I sat next to *Guilt* and *Anger* in the years it took for you to come to grips with the fact that you and your brother were orphans at such a young age. I was with you when you walked away from *Faith*, swearing to never again set foot in a church. And then, I was there with you when you found *Faith* again. Thanks to a wonderful woman who became your wife, with her help, you found your faith again.

And then, oh, you were so into it; you went all in! You wrote a book about *Faith*, became a chaplain, and then went to seminary. You wouldn't even entertain the thought of me in your life during those years. You thought seminary would be all about how to talk to people about God, memorizing creeds and prayers, and learning all about how wonderful God is. What you didn't expect was all the academic work that had to be done before getting to the good stuff, as you called it. And it was during that academic work that I slowly came back into your life.

I've been in your thoughts as you've remembered so many tragic calls from your days as a paramedic and then as a cop.

248

Thirty years of witnessing some of the worst things anyone could imagine would take their toll on anyone. And yet, even with all that crap as a part of your experiences, you decided to become an ordained minister. Maybe it's because you've lived and experienced pain that you feel you can identify with the pain people feel when they come to you. Maybe, because of an orphan disease, it's the physical pain you're in every day that causes you to believe you have a unique sense of empathy you wouldn't otherwise have had. And maybe you've allowed your mind to be opened so you consider things without the need for having all the answers.

Defense:

But, *Doubt*, how do you know all these things about me?

Doubt:

Because I've been there with you during each and every moment. I know you and I know all about you. With all the high-priced criminal defense lawyers I could have hired, why do you think I chose you to represent me?

Defense:

I've been wondering that since I first took your call.

Doubt:

I knew if I was to have any chance of being exonerated, I would need a surprise witness. And I knew you would be the witness I needed to conclude my trial. After all, who knows more about me than you?

Okay, Your Honor. I'm done with my examination of this witness. He can go back to asking me questions again.

The Court:

Well, that was unprecedented.

All right, Counselor, where do you want to take it from here?

Defense:

I just have one more question, Your Honor. It's how I planned on concluding my questioning of *Doubt* before you allowed – I mean, before this unprecedented type of testimony.

Doubt, your accusers say that you are no good for the Church. They've blamed you for a whole slew of things from declining congregations to churches closing their doors. I believe it's important for the jury to hear your answer to this question: Do you want to see the Church fold? Has it been your purpose all along to cause the Church to collapse?

Doubt:

Nothing could be further from the truth! Not only do I *not* want to see the Church fold, I want it to prosper. And not only do I *not* want to see the Church collapse, I want to see it built back up so that it's relevant again. I also want to add that I am not present in the world to make anyone stop believing anything that has anything to do with their faith.

While it can certainly be argued that the Church has made mistakes since its inception – very bad mistakes – it can also be argued that the Church has been a great asset throughout its history. Some of the greatest minds in history, some of the most beautiful artwork, some of the most prolific writers, and some of the greatest acts of love have been demonstrated because of the Church. But over the last thirty years or so, something has happened – and it's getting worse every year. Membership and attendance are down,

> *Not only do I not want to see the Church fold, I want it to prosper. And not only do I not want to see the Church collapse, I want to see it built back up so that it's relevant again.*

scandals are on the rise, and the financial sovereignty of what was once a secure institution is on the brink of collapse.

Does the Church really believe that if I'm pushed out of the lives of people, they'll return to the pews? I think if the Church is honest with itself, it would see that I'm not the reason for the situation it finds itself in, nor was I the reason it began. For reasons that can be discussed and debated outside this courtroom, the Church has lost its importance in most societies around the world. And I'm afraid if it doesn't do something soon, the Church is one generation away, two at the most, of becoming completely irrelevant. That would be such a shame on so many levels.

I also happen to think reading the Bible literally is a shame as well. It's when our twenty-first-century minds try to sort out the historical facts from the implausible written in early first-century manuscripts that I tend to show up. When I'm asked the best way to keep me out of the picture when reading the Bible, my response is always the same: Stop reading the ancient Jewish stories literally. Sure, there are facts in them; there are historical events that really did occur. It's been my experience that these facts appear about as often as a movie that's based on a true story. You've all seen the start of a documentary film where there's a statement, usually in white letters against a black background, saying: "The following movie is based in part on actual events." Sometimes that statement reads: "The following film was inspired by actual events."

When we try to hold the writers of the Gospels to the same scrutiny we would when poring over a history book, we do them a disservice. I also think we do the Gospels a disfavor. No one would think of reading Aesop's Fables as being factually accurate – a tortoise and a hare racing one another and being able to talk, to boot! Not that I'm suggesting the books of the Bible be read the same way the fables are read, but we can decide ahead of time to have the mindset that we

251

are going to find the message in each passage. What was the Gospel writer trying to convey about Jesus' message and his character? Remember, the Gospels were not written during the time of Jesus' ministry. The writers of the Gospels were writing forty to seventy years after Jesus died. According to most theologians, they were telling the Jesus story in the only context they knew.

So when someone reads passages from the Gospels with the intent of finding the message, the experience becomes deeper and often faith grows, too. Some people discover the stories in the Bible become deeply moving when they see themselves as one of the characters in them. They ask themselves, "Which person in the story represents me?" Take the parable of the Good Samaritan – some people might see themselves as the victim who was beaten and robbed; other people might see themselves as the priest or the Levite who crossed to the other side of the road to avoid the victim; others connect with the Samaritan who took pity on the victim; maybe others see themselves as the innkeeper who took the victim in after the Samaritan brought him there. The point is, when the stories in the Gospels are read with the intention of finding the message, they come alive in ways we never imagined. Obviously, everyone is free to read the Bible however they wish; these are just my suggestions for those who don't want me showing up when they read the Bible.

Just a quick supplementary comment on that: Whenever I'm asked which character in the Gospel stories I identify with, for some reason, it's always the disciple Thomas.

I'd like to end my testimony the way it began – by stating my purpose in people's lives. My purpose is to give that nudge to get someone to ask a question, to probe a little, to consider another side of an issue. If I was a tool, I think people would see that I have value. But like any tool, if it's misused, it can cause damage. And I'm not denying that I've been misused.

The question I'd ask the jury to consider is this: Haven't other tools been misused? Anger is an emotion that has its value, but there's no one alive who hasn't witnessed it being misused in such a way that it caused harm. The same can be said about humor; when used correctly, it's wonderful, but it can be disastrous when used at the wrong time and in the wrong situation.

All I can ask the members of the jury is to consider the facts as I've testified, and to think about the good that I have done since I entered the world.

Thank you.

Defense:

Thank you, *Doubt*.

Your Honor, the defense rests.

The Court:

Ok.

Doubt, thank you for your testimony, you may step down from the witness stand.

Counselor, is it your intent to present your closing arguments tomorrow morning?

Defense:

Yes, Your Honor; we'll be offering our closing arguments tomorrow.

The Court:

All right, we'll pick it up then when we reconvene tomorrow morning. Court is in recess until tomorrow morning.

Chapter 12:
Closing Arguments

*Keep an Open Mind * Bible Written Over a Period of 1,100 Years * Gospels Written in a Different Language than Jesus Spoke and Decades After He Lived * Manuscripts Changed by Scribes – Accidentally and Intentionally * Paul's Letters * Contradictions in the New Testament * Early Christian Beliefs and Sects * The Spread of Christianity in the First Century * Problematic Passages * Problem of Reading the Bible Literally*

The Court:

Good morning, everyone.

I trust everyone is well rested and prepared for the defense's closing arguments. It's a bit unusual, but if you remember when the prosecution rested, they opted to present their summation immediately after concluding the examination of their witness. So today, the defense will present their closing arguments.

Counselor, are you ready to proceed?

254

Defense:

Yes, Your Honor, we are.

The Court:

Then, if you're ready, the floor is yours.

Defense:

Thank you, Judge.

Ladies and gentlemen of the jury, good morning. I want to first thank you – each one of you. On behalf of my client, I want to thank you for your willingness to listen to the testimony with an open mind. I know at times the testimony seemed methodical, but there was a reason for that. We wanted to be sure that you heard enough evidence to make an informed decision, yet not bore you with every problematic passage, creed, and doctrine associated with the Bible. Had we done that, we would have been here late into the night, every day, for at least a week. And what would that have accomplished?

Sure, we left out passages that some people might have found problematic or improbable. Our goal wasn't to flood you with information; rather, it was to give you a sampling of the issues that are researched by historians, anthropologists, and biblical scholars. I am confident we met that goal, and I'm sure you will leave here knowing more about the Bible than when this trial started.

But our objective wasn't to give you a history lesson. *Doubt* is on trial. This trial is for *Doubt's* life. Our objective is to give you the information you need to reach a decision that finds *Doubt* not guilty of insurrection against the Church. And it's with that objective in mind that I want to take you back to my opening statement.

If you remember, I shared a story with you. It was more than a just story, though; it was a historical account of a man from the first century from a remote part of the Roman Empire. I'd like you to think back to the assumption you made about the story – the person the historical account was about. Each of you assumed I was talking about Jesus. Based on preconceived beliefs, you were easily led to assume I was talking about Jesus instead of Apollonius of Tyana. I'm going to ask you to think about that for a minute. Think about how your beliefs led you to assume something that wasn't the case.

And in this case, the case before you, it can't be stressed enough the importance of an open mind. Your mind – that part of you where opinions are stored, where beliefs are held. That wondrous part of you that evaluates information and then formulates an opinion. I'd like you now to consider the information that has been presented in this trial, the facts *Doubt* testified to. The things you thought you knew or understood about the Bible and the beliefs that came down from the early first century as a result of the books in it.

Now, consider everything new that is being evaluated in that wondrous mind. It's time to recap, so to speak. This is the part of the trial where you're given the opportunity to review the evidence that's been presented.

You heard my client openly and honestly testify to *Doubt's* purpose: to encourage people to question things when there are contradictions or improbabilities, and to investigate and probe deeper. My client testified that his presence is to give that gentle nudge where people are encouraged to use their God-given intelligence to consider things based on facts.

You heard about the ancient beliefs people had during the time the books of the Bible were written, such as their beliefs about reproduction and the solar system. As more facts became available through the centuries, those beliefs changed. Yet the

256

books that would eventually become the Bible were written based on the understandings humankind had at that time.

You learned how the Bible was written over a time span of about 1,100 years; the books of the Bible were written at different times when different things were happening to the Jewish people. Eleven hundred years of writing went into the books of the Bible. It wasn't like the Bible fell from the sky, and collated with each book divided by chapter and verse. You heard how the books of the New Testament even contain forgeries.

Doubt explained how the Gospels were written by men who lived in different parts of the region than where Jesus lived or taught, and how their religious background was completely different than that of the man about whom they were writing – a man they never met and never knew. They wrote the Gospels in a language Jesus didn't speak. And they wrote them based on the oral traditions about Jesus that were handed down by prior generations. The first Gospel wasn't written until at least forty years after Jesus' death, and the last Gospel wasn't written until nearly seventy years after his death.

You learned about the scribes whose job it was to copy the manuscripts that were called the Gospels. These scribes were hired to copy page by page, line by line, word by word, and letter by letter. And you learned how the scribes were only human, and they made mistakes. These mistakes changed, in some places, the meanings of different passages – some of the changes appear to be accidental, while others appear to be intentional. In some places, verses were deleted, and in others, verses were added.

Scribes had to do the copying because of the literacy rate that hovered between 3 and 5 percent in the areas of Jesus' ministry. Scribes weren't the only problem with the books of the New Testament. You heard *Doubt* testify to the scholarly opinion that only seven out of the thirteen letters written by the apostle Paul were undisputedly written by him. Of the other six, at least four have been determined to be forgeries – someone other than Paul wrote them, and then signed his name to them.

Doubt pointed out some of the contradictions in the Bible, and in the New Testament in particular. He explained how these contradictions cannot be reconciled in any way other than theological explanations that rationalize the conflicts. You also heard testimony of the improbabilities as to the historical inaccuracies in the Bible. Again, only through theological explanations can they be rationalized in hopes of being accepted as factual. It needs to be said that theology is the study of the nature of God. Please remember how you have been asked to evaluate the passages that *Doubt* discussed not from a devotional standpoint, but instead through a historical perspective with a critical eye.

You heard testimony on the beliefs of the earliest Christians based on what Jesus preached – a looming cosmic judgment where the righteous would be given eternal life on earth and the evil will be punished with eternal death. Jesus told his disciples he would be the Messiah of this new kingdom that God would put in place, and each one of them would rule one of the twelve tribes of Israel.

You also learned about the different sects that formed soon after Jesus' death – groups that had their own understanding of Jesus and his message, and each one believing they had the right, or orthodox, understanding. You heard how the most powerful group that was formed declared what was orthodox and what was heresy, and how that understanding led to the accepted beliefs about the nature of Jesus.

Doubt explained how early Christianity spread and how different people had different understandings of who Jesus was in relationship to God. Disputes in churches led to debates among early Church fathers. And when the Emperor Constantine converted, Christianity became an accepted religion. Constantine convened a council of bishops to decide once and for all who Jesus was in relationship to God. You now understand how the doctrine of the Trinity came about and was decided on.

You also listened to passages that have been used to harm others, to put them down; passages that have created hatred in the hearts of people claiming to be Christians who go out and persecute other religions and beliefs. And what about those archaic laws and customs? Think of how many of them are broken every day. They were important for that society when they were written but have become outdated with the passing of time.

Testimony from *Doubt* also included the doctrine of substitutionary atonement, as well as a consideration of God's nature and how passages describing God's love clash with other passages describing God's wrath and judgment. You heard *Doubt* testify to the biblical deaths attributed to God, as well as other acts that are anything but loving. God's nature is something *Doubt* discussed, especially the problem of suffering.

Finally, you heard testimony about the problems of reading the Bible literally, where some people take each book and every passage in each book literally. You heard how if the books of the New Testament are read with the intent to learn the message in each passage, a deeper understanding and growth of faith often occurs. Ultimately, the reader experiences a different appreciation of the books that make up the New Testament.

So now what do you do with all this information – all these facts and historical accounts that historians and scholars teach in seminaries and theological schools? All my client can ask of you is to consider what you thought you knew about the New Testament and Christianity before this trial started, and what you now know. And then, think of what it would be like for us if no one in the last two thousand years questioned the status quo. What would Christianity look like if my client wasn't present in the minds of some of the earliest apostles, the early Church fathers, and the leaders who had the courage to push the limits by questioning long-held beliefs about Jesus?

Ladies and gentlemen, you're not being asked to find that my client was present in each one of the problematic passages, the contradictions, and the errors that he testified to. All that's required for you to acquit my client is to find that *Doubt* was present in just one of the examples that were presented in this trial. I am confident that as you sat there through his testimony, at least one of those examples resonated in you, at least one of those examples nudged you, at least one of those examples had you asking questions within your own mind.

During his testimony, *Doubt* shared a quote from a noted theologian of the twentieth century, Frederick Buechner. It was that quote about *Doubt* being the ants in the pants of faith. I'd like to share another quote from arguably the most influential theologian of the twentieth century, Paul Tillich. Tillich once said this about my client: "Doubt isn't the opposite of faith; it is one element of faith."

My client is an element of faith, according to a respected theologian. And if we go outside the theological explanation of my client, consider the words of an American writer whose works have won acclaim from people of all walks of life. Anne Lamott, in her book, *Plan B: Further Thoughts on Faith*, says this about my client: "The opposite of faith is not doubt, but certainty. Certainty is missing the point entirely." In other words, *Doubt* isn't the enemy to faith; instead, *Doubt* sits there waiting to confront certainty.

260

There are a lot of people who feel my client and faith don't mix. But all of us experience my client at some point in their life. Especially when it comes to faith. My client is there in the faith journeys of just about everyone, but *Doubt* is rarely talked about. And if my client is mentioned, it's a negative discussion where my client is told, "You're not welcome in our faith journey."

What if my client helped the faith journeys of others? Think about everything you've heard, all the evidence that's been presented – everything *Doubt* has testified to without one objection from the prosecution. What if *Doubt* could help produce a richer faith? The former pastor who authored more than ninety books, Mark Littleton, says *Doubt* is the fire through which trust passes, but when it's been tried, it comes out as gold. My client can actually help confirm someone's faith!

The Church has blamed *Doubt* for its decline. The truth is, my client isn't the reason for the decline; the reason is because the Church hasn't adapted to the changes in society. My client *wants* the Church to become relevant again. *Doubt* is going so far as to encourage the Church to consider what it needs to do to become what it used to be – a place of significance where people can relate to God in a way that convinces them they are accepted and cherished and loved for who they are.

Finally, I'm asking you to consider this in your deliberations: What would the world be like *without* my client in it? I'm sure there are more than a few defense attorneys who would have advised me not to ask you that question. But as someone who's seen the benefits of it in life, I think it's a question that needs to be asked as this trial comes to a close.

Think of what your life and the lives of people you know would be like without my client in it. Think about the dangers of unquestioned faith in world leaders, the dangers in religions that suppress questions, and the risks associated with blind faith in the actions of others. Imagine experiencing no hesitation or uncertainty in coming to a conclusion or making an important decision – instead, you just see the positives and never consider the risks. Imagine you have no suspicions in any aspect of your daily routines – instead, you accept every person and situation as good, regardless of what others say about them. And imagine believing everything you read and hear is the truth, without hesitation – so you accept that whatever you are told is factual without any errors or flaws.

Maybe you now see the potential dangers of having faith without my client in it. Maybe you're thinking about the damages that have already been done when my client was pushed away at different times in the history of the Church. And perhaps these dangers and damages might even be personal to you.

Now that you've considered the dangers of removing *Doubt* from life, think about the positives of having my client present from time to time. How many times have you personally benefited from asking questions – hesitating before jumping to a conclusion, being suspicious of something or someone, or by paying attention to that feeling inside of you that said, "This doesn't sound right?"

We don't always get answers to our questions. The conclusions we come to aren't always what we expect, we don't always know the reasons we're suspicious, and we don't always find out why something didn't sound right. But we are grateful that we have in us the ability to pause and think before accepting something or doing something or saying something. I don't think any of us would consider that a bad thing.

It's important to remember that people can come up with theological explanations for the problems in the Bible – explanations that resolve contradictions, conflicts, implausible

262

passages, and historical inaccuracies. But these explanations are from a theological perspective. Please remember that you've been asked to consider the evidence with a critical eye. Theology, in its simplest form, is the study of God. This trial is not about God; it is about the issues that are in the only book accepted by the Church that explains God, God's nature, and the Son of God.

I'll leave you with this thought: Maybe faith isn't about having all the answers. There are questions that will never be answered, and that's okay! Having questions and demanding answers are two different things. Growth comes from probing and questioning and reevaluating. A medical student who instead of studying and learning the material was given answers to every test she or he took would not make a very good doctor. It's the process of learning, not just knowing the answers, that turns a medical student into a good doctor, a doctor people have faith in.

As you deliberate, I'm asking you to have faith in *Doubt*.

Thank you.

Chapter 13:
Case Review

So. How did the jury deliberations go? Was *Doubt* acquitted or was *Doubt* sent to the chair?

It's my hope that you enjoyed the defense's presentation of its one and only witness. I also hope you learned something new or had the opportunity to consider facts you already knew, but got to see them in a new light. My goal was to share information that's taught in seminaries and theological schools in a way that's easier to understand than having to sit through hours of bookwork in uncomfortable lecture-hall chairs.

I believe if Christianity is going to survive, the Church needs to make changes that keep it relevant as it treads water in figuring out a game plan. One of those changes must be sharing with laypeople what is known in the academic realm. Maybe the Church is concerned that if laypeople have the same information as the clergy, some kind of imaginary balance of power will be shifted. Or, perhaps the Church is worried that if laypeople have some of the same biblical knowledge, their faith will be negatively impacted; that is to say, their doubts will have them questioning centuries-old traditions and doctrines.

Dispelling the Myth of a Vengeful God – And Confronting a Family Dynamic

Whatever the reason, the Church must adapt to the challenges of twenty-first-century thinking and needs. Twenty-first-century people have needs that differ greatly from the people for whom the Bible was originally written, because they have a different understanding of the world and the universe. They've seen that all the threats of a vengeful God handed down through the generations haven't come to fruition. And yet, many still hold on to the fear of God the Father being angry with them or not loving or forgiving them if they don't worship God. Yes, fear and guilt do wonders in keeping people in line.

This might be a good place to offer a trigger warning for anyone who has suffered abuse in their family. Even though people see the dissonance, they still hold on to old beliefs. Most twenty-first-century Christians are able to see past the idea that, as children of God, they are in a figurative family where they are reminded constantly that they aren't worthy of much and can't do much of anything right. The father of this family tells them this constantly. This father also insists that he loves his children very much. Over time, these children come to see themselves as worthless and develop a perverted idea of what parental love is. As a way of reinforcing this family dynamic, the father insists on a ritual where once a week the children gather and tell the father what they've done wrong – everything they screwed up and everything they should have done, but didn't. They tell the father they're sorry and ask for his forgiveness. The father tells them that he can only forgive them if they believe he loves them.

Most Christians see past this neurotic family dynamic. And yet, they hold onto the hope that might come from it. As adults, they know this kind of family situation is psychological abuse, but they're afraid to lose their father's love. And as adults, many are stuck at the maturity level of seeing themselves as having little worth without the father's involvement and being dependent on his advice and reassurance. Unfortunately, this leads to low self-esteem where they don't love themselves in a healthy way. Without the father there to be showered with love, they find it hard to love themselves, and even others.

Understanding the History of the Bible and the Context in Which It Was Written

What's been shared in the pages of this book is just a fraction of what is learned by those who've made a decision to devote their lives to the Church or to studying Christianity. This trial of my friend and constant companion *Doubt* highlighted some of the history of Christianity so that we can better understand how we got to where we're at.

Stories that were told in the first century that turned Jesus the Christ into a mystical savior have become the basis for worshipping the Christ instead of following the teachings of Jesus. The development of the tradition of Jesus being the fully human, yet fully divine, sacrifice became the doctrine of substitutionary atonement. Passages cherry-picked by some denominations have been used as a reason to exclude others, or at the very least, make them feel less than welcome.

In our time here, in this present time we're living in, we have different understandings of nature, of the universe, and of humanity than what was known when the books of the Bible were written. Maybe the conflict people feel is from being asked to force ancient beliefs and ideas to fit the knowledge they possess today. Or, maybe the conflict they feel is from being asked to toss out everything they know to be true about the universe and all it contains in order to be accepted into the Church.

Opening Hearts and Honoring Doubts

Instead of a literal reading of the books of the New Testament, what if people gathered regularly, say, once a week, to talk about the teachings of Jesus? What if open discussions were encouraged, what if questions were encouraged? What if people's doubts were honored?

Knowing what you know now compared to what you may not have known, or considered, before the trial started, think about how the questions in the previous paragraph could ignite a renewed interest by those who have left the Church. That can also be said about those who've been curious about Christianity, but have never felt drawn to a typical church. Heck, I'm willing to bet it can also be said about those who identify as atheist or agnostic. I often wonder how all of us – Christian and Jew, Muslim and Buddhist, fundamentalist and atheist, citizen and immigrant – would benefit if the Church's teachings included the understanding that we are all interconnected.

> *I often wonder how all of us – Christian and Jew, Muslim and Buddhist, fundamentalist and atheist, citizen and immigrant – would benefit if the Church's teachings included the understanding that we are all interconnected.*

Since my ordination, I've been wondering how the Church would benefit if it encouraged its clergy to share more than theological discussions of the sacred texts. I'm not suggesting that on Sunday mornings, from the pulpit, ministers across the country begin talking about the problems in the manuscripts that made their way into the pages of the New Testament. Something happens when you speak from the pulpit; it's not so much that you feel you're speaking for God, but it's how those sitting in pews see you. Since childhood, it's been an unspoken understanding that the person speaking from the pulpit has a special authority that is not questioned.

Instead of from the pulpit, Bible studies could be offered to interested congregants. In that setting, outside the holiness of the sanctuary, topics such as those addressed in this book could be discussed. Questions could be asked. Feelings could be shared. And doubt could be embraced instead of pushed aside as some kind of unwelcomed intruder.

I'd like to imagine the Church as an institution that welcomes not just the sinners, but sinners who also have questions – serious questions about the books that make up the New Testament. I'd like to imagine the Church that welcomes sinners with doubts – doubts that are encouraged to be shared in a trusting atmosphere. And I'd like to imagine a church that supports its clergy when they find the courage to share what they learned – not just the theological stuff, but critical assessments of the sacred texts we call The Bible.

Experiencing the Messages in the Bible

Maybe it's only after we stop reading the Bible literally that we can take it seriously. We can seriously look at the passages in the Gospels and gain an understanding of the messages and the meaning of them. We can seriously look at our own beliefs about Jesus and see how they stack up against the picture the writers of the Gospels attempted to portray. And when we're ready, we can seriously contemplate, and experience, the teachings of Jesus.

> *Maybe it's only after we stop reading the Bible literally that we can take it seriously.*

Then we can allow ourselves to wonder about the original mission of Jesus – his parables, his conviction, and even his suffering and his death. We can wonder what the disciples experienced after his death that turned them from frightened cowards who hid during his crucifixion into brave apostles who were willing to give up their lives in order to have the message of Jesus spread far and wide.

As an agnostic, I have struggles with much of the Bible. The trial depicted in this book exposed most of them. But just as the Bible doesn't define my identity, my struggles don't prevent me from experiencing the messages that Jesus taught – the messages Jesus left for us to consider. These struggles, as strange as this might sound, allow me to read from a place of wonderment the messages of each passage in the Gospels. Instead of from a place of righteousness, from that place where I used to read them, I find that I now *experience* the teachings of Jesus.

Typically, a minister answers questions from her or his congregation. As an agnostic minister, I find I have more questions

268

than answers. I sometimes curse myself and regret that I ever began deeper research into the New Testament. Had I just been content with where I was, I never would have pursued my doctorate. Had I just left well enough alone and moved on with ministry after my ordination, I doubt very much I'd be facing the struggles that I face. The deconstructing of my former beliefs was one of the most painful experiences of my life. And like I said, there are times I've regretted opening the can of worms that gave me a different understanding of my faith.

But there are times – many more than the times of regret – when I rejoice at the freedom I feel in knowing that dogma and doctrines no longer have a hold on my faith. I traded my old transactional theology for a *transformational faith*. I'm now free to have a relationship with the Divine in ways that I never knew existed. And although that freedom came at a price, I am grateful I found it.

> *I traded my old transactional theology for a transformational faith. I'm now free to have a relationship with the Divine in ways that I never knew existed.*

Finding Gratitude and the Freedom to Soar

And I'm grateful to experience it every day with someone who recklessly uttered two words that changed for the better my life and the life of my two boys, Corey and Matt. My wife Elissa said, "I do," more than twelve years ago. Little did she know that about a year and a half after our wedding, she would become my caregiver. Just after Thanksgiving of that year, I was diagnosed with a tumor in my spinal cord. After visits to several hospitals and different neurosurgeons, one description of my situation was constant: This tumor is considered inoperable and untreatable. It's not malignant, thank God; but as it grows, it's slowing killing the nerves that control my legs.

As she was proofreading this final chapter, Elissa reminded me of something I'd forgotten due to the fog caused by both the tumor pain and the lasting effects of my latest concussion. (I've had at least five concussions since my diagnosis and this book was written while recuperating from the worst one yet.) Elissa reminded me that although my legs aren't working the way they used to, that hasn't stopped me from soaring. When I told her I was stuck on how to end this book, she looked at me and said, "Jonathan Livingston Seagull."

Elissa knows it is my favorite book. During the beginning phase of this book, in addition to researching the books of the New Testament for what seemed like the umpteenth time, I read for the third time *Jonathan Livingston Seagull.*

A few paragraphs ago, I mentioned the freedom I now have after being released from the conformity of religion. In order to soar, Jonathan Seagull had to leave behind the conformity of staying close to the shore with the rest of the flock; he had to find the courage to push beyond the boundaries of what he had been told gulls do and had always done; he had to endure the guilt and sadness of being banished from the flock for his decision to go against the status quo of what's expected from a gull; and Jonathan Seagull had to be willing to risk losing his life as he knew it so he could find the life that was waiting for him to discover.

Jonathan Livingston Seagull discovered the freedom that came from listening to his own voice – freedom that allowed him to soar like no gull had ever soared before. Doubt didn't hold him back; rather, it gave him opportunities to question things that turned an ordinary seagull into an inspiration, and one of the best-selling books of all time.

My hope and my prayer is – like Jonathan Livingston Seagull – you too might soar.

Recommended Reading

Armstrong, Karen. *The Bible: A Biography (Books That Changed the World)*. New York: Atlantic Monthly Press, 2006.

Armstrong, Karen. *The Lost Art of Scripture: Rescuing the Sacred Texts*. New York and Toronto: Alfred A. Knopf, 2019.

Borg, Marcus. *Evolution of the Word: The New Testament in the Order the Books Were Written*. New York: HarperCollins Publishers, 2012.

Borg, Marcus. *Reading the Bible Again for the First Time: Taking the Bible Seriously but Not Literally*. New York: HarperCollins Publishers, 2001.

Ehrman, Bart D. *How Jesus Became God: The Exaltation of a Jewish Preacher from Galilee*. New York: HarperCollins Publishers, 2014.

Ehrman, Bart D. *Jesus Interrupted: Revealing the Hidden Contradictions in the Bible (And Why We Don't Know About Them)*. New York: HarperCollins Publishers, 2009.

Ehrman, Bart D. *Lost Christianities: The Battles for Scripture and the Faiths We Never Knew*. New York: Oxford University Press, 2003.

Ehrman, Bart D. *Misquoting Jesus: The Story Behind Who Changed the Bible and Why.* New York: HarperCollins Publishers, 2005.

Evans, Rachel Held. *Searching for Sunday: Loving, Leaving, and Finding the Church.* Nashville, TN: Nelson Books, 2015.

Spong, John Shelby. *Biblical Literalism: A Gentile Heresy: A Journey into a New Christianity Through the Doorway of Matthew's Gospel.* New York: HarperCollins Publishers, 2016.

Spong, John Shelby. *Re-Claiming the Bible for a Non-Religious World.* New York: HarperCollins Publishers, 2011.

Spong, John Shelby. *Rescuing the Bible from Fundamentalism: A Bishop Rethinks the Meaning of Scripture.* New York: HarperCollins Publishers, 1991.

Spong, John Shelby. *Why Christianity Must Change or Die: A Bishop Speaks to Believers in Exile.* New York: HarperCollins Publishers, 1998.

Taylor, Barbara Brown. *Leaving Church: A Memoir of Faith.* New York: HarperCollins Publishers, 2006.

Bolz-Weber, Nadia. *Accidental Saints: Finding God in All the Wrong People.* New York: Penguin Random House/Convergent Books, 2015.

Wells, Steve. *The Skeptic's Annotated Bible.* SAB Books, 2012.

Index

273

B

C

D

276

E

F

J

K

L

M

Q

R

S

U

V

W

Y

Z

About the Author

Rusty Williams is the author of two previous books: *Can I Get There From Here: One Cop's Irreverent Look at Faith*; and *Pee, Poop, Heartache, and Love: Life Lessons Learned From Fostering Shelter Dogs.* Ordained into the Christian Ministry in 2008, Rusty holds a Master of Divinity degree in Pastoral Counseling and a Doctor of Ministry degree in Church Development. A former youth minister, Rusty was diagnosed in 2009 with a rare disease (a spinal cord tumor) that has left him disabled. He now devotes his time to healing both his mind and body. Through the practices of self-hypnosis and mindfulness, he is able to work through many of the debilitating effects of the disease.

Rusty has spent his entire adult life helping others. Before starting a 25-year career as a highly decorated police officer (retiring as a detective), Rusty entered a paramedic training program right out of high school and became the youngest paramedic to be certified in his state. During his tenure in both professions, he was an instructor and board member for state organizations and he presented workshops around the country. Now, as a clinical hypnotist, Rusty works with people to help them overcome challenges in their lives. He is an internationally known hypnosis instructor and a former producer and host of a national weekly radio show on mindfulness and hypnosis.

Rusty considers himself to be the luckiest guy in the world: He is the father of two amazing young men, Matt and Corey, and the husband of a beautiful woman, Elissa, who deserves sainthood! Because of his disability, gravity and Rusty have a love-hate relationship. His children and wife have picked him up when he was down – both literally and figuratively – more times than he can count, and he is forever grateful they are in his life. He and Elissa love spending time with their two dogs and enjoying the possibilities waiting around every corner of this journey called life.

In 2014, Rusty and Elissa started the Barefoot Ministries to help others who are suffering, either physically or spiritually. To learn more about that ministry, or to read the discussion questions about this book, please visit TheBarefootMinistries.org.

Made in the USA
Middletown, DE
12 May 2021